—————— DREAM DEFE(

"Finally a devotional for the entrepreneurial-go-get-em-lets-do-stuff kind of ladies! It's refreshing and inspiring!"

PROMISE TANGEMAN, Founder and designer of : Go Live HQ

"If you have ever experienced the burden of a dream, and then the sheer joy of that burden being carried by our God of amazing grace, you know the power of prayers prayed in faithful surrender. This beautiful collection of guided prayers is an invitation to walk with God on the journey of surrendering to the dreams He's given us. Jenn and Kelly have walked the walk, so they can talk the talk. They offer heartfelt, authentic, and relevant encouragement for fellow dreamers and doers. These pages of courageous, vulnerable prayers are exactly what the dreamer in me needed. It's time to wake up the creative God designed us to be, and to say yes to the God-given God-sized dreams in our hearts."

ERYN HALL, Declare Conference

"Praying and reading God's word are things that I do not do with any regularity. I avoid these things out of fear. Fear of doing it wrong, of being vulnerable, of the changes that letting God really, truly into my life and heart will bring. This book took me gently by the hand and heart and reminded me that I'm going to be okay. It gave me a safe place to open myself up to Christ's love and leading. I feel encouraged and empowered. This book will take you through vulnerable and uncomfortable topics and, with grace and care, give you the space to open yourself up to becoming the beautiful, brave, and bold woman that God always knew you could be. Now it's time to believe in you. You can do it, sweet one."

STEPHANIE KILPER, Dreamer and Builder

"Finally! The prayers my heart has whispered all along have been captured in one place. Jenn and Kelly know what a Dreamer and Doer face on a daily basis and this book y'all! I'll be keeping it within arm's reach for those moments I need to be reminded that God hears my petitions. This book reminds me to rest in identity and have faith as I steward my calling and business."

SARAH HARMEYER, Neighbors Table

"Jenn Sprinkle has been lifting me up, championing my dreams, and holding my hand in prayer for many years. It's no surprise to me that she would create a book that would do the same. Thirty-One Days of Prayer for the Dreamer and the Doer will not only inspire you, it will light a fire, fuel your passion, and give you purpose."

ROBIN YEAGER, Co-Founder of Mailagrams
and Managing Editor of Society Bride

"The battle between dreaming and doing is real. I think of myself as primarily a doer, not a dreamer, but the truth is I struggle with both. I'm good at getting the immediate stuff done but awful at taking the time to dream about what could be. And sure, I have these latent dreams (I like to call them "ideas") but I don't really think that I could actually do something to make them happen. I love the idea of a resource that encourages and inspires women to actually slow down and pray to the God of the universe who supplies both the dream and the power to do. May God-inspired dreams come true for our great joy and His great glory as a result of this book!"

DAPHNE BAMBURG, daphnebamburg.com

"For years, I fell into the category of "surviving" not "dreaming." I'm mom to a little girl plagued with trauma and am simultaneously battling a chronic disease. So, I pretty much gave up on my dreams. But, God wanted more for me. This book could not have come at a more perfect time in my process with my ministry. I wept reading the chapter on fear and comparison. There are days I wake up and think "nope, I can't do it today" and will list 100 ways I am failing. It is so easy to forget that this is ALL God's...this is not about me. It's a daily surrender, and I ultimately just want to love people and Jesus more. This book is a gift on my journey, so full of truth and encouragement."

LINDSEY WHEELER, Bottle of Tears

"This book is a must for all women who dream of living their life on purpose and for a purpose. I wish I had it when I was remembering how to dream and writing my first book. Thirty-One Days of Prayer for the Dreamer and Doer is soaked in wisdom, truth, and grace. I will be using it again and again as I walk this path that God has called me to. Thank you, girls for pouring your heart and soul out onto these pages."

CORIE CLARK, The Simplicity Project

"Jenn and Kelly prove themselves to be kindred-spirits by authentically sharing their own dreamer struggles. They truly understand my swirling head, so full of thoughts and ideas I often forget to include God in my conversations. This treasure of a book holds the antidote to this dreamer's dilemma by spoon-feeding beautiful prayers and scriptures to my weary soul. The penetrating questions to reflect on, propel me forward and remind me God won't let me settle!"

SHARON MANKIN, Bless Your Neighbor

"This book is such an encouragement to anyone who wants to strengthen their walk with God! The prayers and devotions cover all the subjects that we want to seek God with concerning our work, family, and dreams. This gives us the words when sometimes we can't put words to our heart's cries. Thank you so much to all the brave, inspiring women who share their hearts and prayers to help us in our daily walk. This book will be part of our devotional time for years to come!!"

TRACE AND JENI MAJOR, dream defenders

"As I read, I thought, 'How did they know what I was going through?' Because we are often building and dreaming in isolation, it can feel like you're the only one but you're not. I celebrate the transparency of the authors. As a business owner who walks women through discovering and building their God-given dreams, I know these prayers will be a resource for all of us as we juggle many roles. Along with my Bible, I'll continue to run to these prayers when I'm feeling empty and even when my cup is full."

MICHELLE MCKINNEY, Dreams Unleashed

THIRTY ONE DAYS OF

PRAYER

THE —— FOR —— THE
dreamer + doer

BY JENN SPRINKLE + KELLY RUCKER
and friends of THE {WELL} STUDIO

foreward by Jennie Allen // *afterword by Lara Casey*

PRAYERS . SCRIPTURE . DEVOTIONAL

Published by:
NyreePress Literary Group
P.O. Box 164882
Fort Worth, TX 76161
www.nyreepress.com

ISBN print: 978-0-9909652-5-1
ISBN e-book: 978-0-9909652-6-8
Library of Congress Control Number: 2014957424

Christian Living / Inspirational / Prayer

friends in the trenches

I feel at home with dreamers. I feel understood with dreamers. I find my insanity is sane with dreamers. I find my courage with dreamers.

This is our place, friends—a book full of our people. A book full of cries and prayers and hopes that will feel so familiar and so refreshing. We need each other, and we need God.

My twelve-year-old daughter is quite the artist. I could only ever dream of creating beauty the way she does with charcoal and watercolors. But as I watch her passions and talents grow, the discouragement in her own mind only seems to get louder. I want more than anything to protect her from it, and yet I am so familiar with the internal struggle to create.

The deeper we go into the rabbit hole of our imaginations and the braver the work, the more resistance we face.

Jenn Sprinkle has been a soul sister and fellow dreamer for a couple of decades now. She has always nodded yes when so many others looked at me confused; she has grieved with me at rejection and cried with joy when my dreams have come true. She and Kelly are the kind of friends you want in your trenches when the bombs are going off overhead or within your head— the kind of friends who won't let you stop but aren't afraid to tell you how you have gotten off course.

This project is Jenn and Kelly and all of us in the trenches with you. This is us calling out to God together for fresh perspective and courage and perseverance. This is us praying for revival in our own hearts so that we may spark flames of it in others, whether you are designing a home or creating lyrics or birthing a novel. We are all fighting the same fights. We are all fighting the resistance to create.

God is the creator of creatives, and this tribe of fellow creators here all believe that we work with Him on our projects. It is through Him, with Him, for Him and because of Him that we build and dream and create!

God, stir and move us. We are yours.

JENNIE ALLEN
AUTHOR OF ANYTHING and RESTLESS

WHEN GOD BIRTHS A BURDEN IN YOUR HEART,
LEAN INTO IT.

-ANDY STANLEY-

SHE DESIGNS A LIFE FULL OF DREAMS
ONLY ONE CAN FULFILL
SHE FINDS VALUE IN BEING HIS INSTEAD OF BEING BUSY
HER PASSION IS CONTAGIOUS
SHE MEASURES HERSELF IN STRENGTH, NOT POUNDS
SHE TRUSTS THE STRUGGLE
AND BREATHES IN THE JOY OF THE JOURNEY
HER STORY IS ONE TO BE HEARD
SHE RUNS FROM COMPARISON INTO THE
ARMS OF CONFIDENCE
SHE TURNS HER BACK ON PERFECTION AND

she chooses grace

-JENN SPRINKLE-

the burden of a dream

BY JENN SPRINKLE

Dream big.

Pursue your dreams.

Stop wishing. Start doing.

Do what you love.

The dream is free. The hustle is sold separately.

Good things happen to those who hustle.

We hear it all the time. The pep talks. The motivation to go out there and make our dreams come true. We hustle, we succeed, we cry, we rejoice, we fail, we dream, we do. The life of a dreamer can look so inspiring and so beautiful and so full of adventure.

And it is.

And then it isn't.

And then it is again.

I took the StrengthsFinder test a few years ago. I love taking these kinds of tests, because someone else is telling me what my strengths are and what I should do instead of me trying to figure it all out myself. My number one strength was Futuristic. That is the only strength I can remember all of these years later, so I thought I would go back and look up what it meant again.

Futuristic says:

You are a dreamer who sees visions of what could be and who cherishes those visions.

My action items are to:

Choose roles in which you can contribute your ideas about the future. For example, you might excel in entrepreneurial or start-up situations. Take time to think about the future. The more time you spend considering your ideas about the future, the more vivid your ideas will become. The more vivid your ideas, the more persuasive you will be.

Apparently, I am a dreamer to my core. Anyone who knows me can attest to this; it is definitely who God made me. Then there is my calling, what I have been uniquely gifted and called by the Lord to walk out in my life. Then there is my purpose and why I am on this earth, which is to share the hope of salvation and bring glory to God in all that I do. For me, this is where the wrestling begins. How do I dream well within my calling and purpose?

As a graphic designer and creative strategist, my job is to help businesses with their branding and online space. Having Futuristic as my strength comes in handy when helping my clients build their dreams. The creative strategy part is definitely what fires me up. Over the years,

I have had the privilege of sitting across from so many women while listening intently to their stories—stories of joyful success and weary struggles, brilliant dreams and scary risks, inspiring ideas and fears of failure.

My heart was burdened.

I was sitting in church one Sunday a couple of years ago, and the charge was given to find a ministry you can connect with. It had been a long time since I had been intentional about a specific ministry, and it was time. My husband and I knew we were called to serve in marriage ministry, but the Lord revealed something else to me that day. He said, *"This community you feel a burden for, THEY need community."* It was my community…my people….the dreamers and the doers, the hustlers and the risk takers. *"They need community,"* He said.

I was called.

That week I dreamed of what it would look like, and I knew I didn't want to do it alone. I wanted someone to walk out this calling with. So I approached my friend, Kelly and said, "I know you are going to think I am crazy, but I have ANOTHER idea." Kelly is one of those friends who is a dream defender and I knew we shared the same burden for this community. Thankfully, she didn't think I was crazy, and The {well} Studio was born—a community of dreamers and doers who love Jesus.

Find community. Find your #dreamdefenders.

I would love to say that this is where the inspiration, beauty, and adventure of the dream began. But friends, I ran ahead of God, became paralyzed, got caught up in comparison, and grew weary and fearful.

> God gives us a vision, and then He takes us down to the
> valley to batter us into the shape of that vision.
> Every God-given vision will become real
> if we only have patience.
> -OSWALD CHAMBERS-

The Lord gave us a vision, and that vision birthed a lot of dreams. Big dreams. Months and months were spent filling pages and pages with ideas, thoughts, and plans. We were so excited and so full of energy.

And yet so paralyzed. For over a year.

After the vision came and the dreams were birthed, we hosted a successful launch party and then I quickly began comparing what I felt like the Lord had called me to do to other people's callings, gifts, and talents. I started looking around and saying, *"Well 'she' is doing something similar and is super successful already. Why should I even start?"* As I walked through a season of comparison, Kelly challenged me to physically disconnect from the online distractions and said to me in her sweet and firm way, *"God doesn't call just one of us."* Such truth. My friend Casey reminded me that *"His kingdom is big enough for all of us."* I had friends speaking truth and keeping me in my lane.

> Never compare your beginning to someone else's middle.
> -JON ACUFF-

Its important to have one or two friends in your life who support your crazy dreams, pick you up when you are weary, and cheer you on in your dream journey. Not everyone will get it, and some people will think you are crazy. That is okay. Not everyone is a dreamer.

So I prayed.

I would like to say that this is where I got back on track, but the ideas were so many, I didn't know where to start. I was trying to sort through which ones were my desires and which ones were God's.

While The {well} Studio dreams and ideas poured in I was still running a design business that had me working at least full days, sometimes late into the evening. So when I shared this vision of The {well} Studio with my husband, his initial fears were valid. It was a challenge already to make time and energy for us after a long workday. *(If you are a business owner, you know what I mean.)* I was adding another dream to the pile of already demanding projects. Our marriage had already suffered in the past due to my hustling. I couldn't afford to build anything that would compromise our marriage again.

Don't let the hustle take over your home.

So I prayed.

I watched God turn Jon's fears into support, and he began to dream with me. I felt free to move forward. The details of building a business rushed in like a flood. What does it look like? How often do we blog? What content do we write? Do we monetize? Do we sell product? What product do we sell? I was growing weary, and we had barely begun. *"Remember that moment in church? Remember your "why"? You were called that day. Keep going."*

Physically document the day God revealed to you His unique calling for you and your "why".
In times of discouragement you will need come back to it.

It was time to create a message, branding, and a website. The message and branding came quickly to both of us: work, live and love well, *not perfectly but {well}*. I didn't seem to take our motto to heart, because when it came to the website, I picked that thing to death. I was waiting for it to be perfect. Waiting. And waiting.

So I prayed.

I will say it again. Have friends in your life who will keep you in your lane. After a year of paralyzing fear, comparison, distractions, overwhelming ideas, exhaustion, and a drive for perfection, Kelly said, *"Let's keep it simple."*

Don't wait for perfect. Go ugly early.

And we did. We closed the notebook of ideas and set them aside, and I remember the Lord saying, *"I just asked you to create a community. I will give back the ideas and dreams when it's time."* We had already run ahead of Him and launched this brand too early a year before with grandiose ideas and no execution. Fail. So here we were again—everything stripped down to a simple site and a simple community. And finally The {well} Studio began to grow.

The End. *Not quite.*

You know how people say they have a "fear of success"? I used to not understand this. How could one fear success? I get it now. I see how the world gets caught up in success and numbers and gets lost in it all. I didn't want that. How would we grow this community God called us to grow but not get lost in it? Then I heard Jess Connolly share one time: *"Grow His Kingdom, not yours. You will mess up, you will get lost, but when you do, choose grace and then keep going."*

Done. I was going to choose grace.

Choose Grace. Often.

I humbly share that most of that wrestling took place over the course of a year. A YEAR! A year lost? *Maybe.* Or maybe a lost year that the Lord was choosing to redeem, inspire, and build something bigger than us.

This book. This book was birthed out of this season of wrestling with a calling God gave us and the dreams that followed. He is the Dream Giver.

And we know that God causes all things to work together for good to those who love God, to those who are called according to His purpose.

Romans 8:28 (NIV)

If you ever feel unworthy to dream or receive the abundant blessings the Lord has in store for you, stop. Because Jesus saw you worthy to die on the cross for and He sees you worthy to bless.

Whether you are called to design, create, write, speak, support, grow, share, serve, or build...there will be a journey. There will be days of joy, days of weariness, days of fear, days of success, days of loss, days of restoration, days of creativity, days of brokenness, days of rest, and days of nothing.

Whatever the day, stay tethered to the Dream Giver with prayer and His Word. We desire for these prayers to bring hope, conviction, encouragement, and guidance as you answer the call and hold your dreams with an open hand.

Dreaming is a beautiful burden that can bring ultimate glory to the Dream Giver.

a call to surrender

BY KELLY RUCKER

The heartbeat of The {well} Studio is splashed upon the pages of this book. Each prayer belongs to a woman who is so in love with God, passionate about His work, compassionate for His people, and so desperate for His presence, all while wrestling through their own "dream journey." Jenn and I could have poured our hearts into each prayer on these pages, but from the beginning we knew that wasn't what the Lord desired for this project. One of the scriptures that we base our mission on is Matthew 25:21, *"The master said, 'Well done, my good and faithful servant. You have been faithful in handling this small amount, so now I will give you many more responsibilities. Let's celebrate together!'" (NLT)*. Together. This is what we saw. Women coming together, celebrating together, praying together, and encouraging together. It's been a beautiful thing to be a part of.

When compiling the content for this book, Jenn and I carefully thought about the different prayers a dreamer might pray. We asked God to lay on our hearts the specific women He wanted to write each prayer and to inspire their words. What happened next was so affirming. Several of them shared with us that their prayer was the very area they were wrestling with. It was not a coincidence. We knew God was orchestrating this project to be pure, authentic, and full of integrity.

These prayers are God inspired and the reflection of women desperate for Him. Though these prayers are personal, these prayers belong to YOU.

As a new mom, I find myself in a season of life that is so foreign. My world has changed in every way. There is so much joy in this season, but if I'm honest there is also doubt and fear. I'm taking it day by day. During the last trimester of my pregnancy, I found myself spending more time in His presence, seeking His counsel, and praying that He would lead me. I knew there were big changes ahead, and I doubted myself. Will I be a good mom? Will I be the wife my husband needs? Will my business still thrive? Will I lose myself? These are the questions I asked myself daily.

To be honest, I struggled with what to say in my chapter on Seasons. This new season of motherhood has me in a bit of a fog. How fitting that my prayer is on seasons—the area in my life where I'm most desperate for God. The Lord has been working in my heart and encouraging me to just be present in the moment, no matter how exhausted I might be. I realize how much I need him in the day to day, not just in this season, but in every season to come. I can't do it without Him, nor do I want to.

It's imperative that I stay in His presence daily. Otherwise, I tend to wander and stray. My thoughts go to a negative place, and my love for people can be very sparse. I tend to rush through the days and sometimes find myself living in survival mode. I need Him deeply. While writing my chapter, I felt Him calling me to surrender. He may even be calling you to surrender. After all, it's not by chance that you have this book in your hands. He is pursuing you. When we lay down our own agenda, our plans and our fears, He gives us peace with new perspective and builds our faith. I pray that as you read through each prayer in this book it will create an atmosphere of worship in your heart and a call to surrender in your life.

He longs to know you.

> Trust in the Lord with all your heart and lean not on your
> own understanding; in all your ways surrender to him,
> and he will make your paths straight.
> Proverbs 3:5-6 (NIV)

I asked, *"God, what do you want me to share?"* He reminded me to choose transparency and grace...not perfection. That is our mission for {well}: allowing grace for ourselves and generously giving it to others.

Each of these prayers represents a season in our lives. Whether you are struggling with comparison, are in the trenches of motherhood, fighting for your marriage, or navigating a new business idea...He is right there with you.

We pray this book is a source of encouragement and a call to action. Feel free to write in the margins and doodle on the pages. There are no rules. In addition, we have created a prayer journal for you to pen your thoughts, answer the questions, and pour out whatever inspires you. We get our best ideas when we are in His presence and inspired by the Holy Spirit. Meditate on each prayer as long or as little as you want. Dwell on each chapter for one day or one month—whatever you feel led to do. We want this book to be a place of meditation and surrender in your life.

• Jot down prayer requests in the margin of the page as you read
• Record dates that prayers were answered and dreams were birthed
• Gather your fellow dream defenders, pray, and discuss the questions
• Repeat every month. Prayers change, answers change, dreams change.

While some of the prayers may not be applicable to you (e.g., motherhood, singleness, business) and while they are written in the voice of each contibutor, we pray that this devotional as a whole will meet you where you are.

Dear Heavenly Father,

We lift up Your daughter to You right now, the one reading the prayers on these pages. Lord, we ask that in the days to come, You would affirm the calling and purpose You have designed for her. Encourage her, defend her, and equip her. Where there is doubt or question about her destiny, how You have gifted her and what You have called her uniquely to for Your glory, reveal to her with clarity...in a loud voice or even a soft whisper. And at the end of the day as she wrestles within this "dream journey" that You have set her on, may she choose grace every day—the grace you died to give that covers our sins and saves us for an eternity with You. Lord, where she may doubt or question this grace, I pray for clarity in your word and through Your people. In Your name we pray, amen.

the prayers

—— 1 ——
PRAYER

May I never forget
just how much prayer
changes, not only my
circumstances, but my
heart too.

Father,

I ask for your hand to guide me through this day. May your name always be on my lips. Give me wisdom and discipline to choose prayer over less important things that so easily distract me. When I forget, bring me back to you. May I never forget just how much prayer changes not only my circumstances but my heart.

I pray my prayers would not be empty words that I repeat just because I know it's good to do, but that I would believe with all my heart that prayer to YOU, the one and only true God, is a powerful thing. And when I have a tendency to make prayer like rubbing a magic lamp, draw me back to your truth.

I pray you would work outside my little box of what I anticipate from life. You see so much more than I can see in any circumstance. Teach me how to start each day with hope of what you have in store, and fill me with the courage to pray bold prayers in light of a deep, abounding faith and hope in you.

Let me not forget all those people around me! Though I may not be able to fill every need that arises, lay people on my heart today who need to be wrapped in prayer and your love.

For those requests that I grow weary praying for every day with no answer, give me patience for your glorious timing and remind me that your view of my circumstance is vastly bigger than my own. For those requests that are answered with a no, let it not shake my faith; instead, help me to dig deep knowing you have something better in mind.

Thank you, Lord, for the beauty of getting to chat with you each and every day.

———————

I patiently waited, Lord, for you to hear my prayer. You listened.
Psalm 40:1 (CEV)

Don't fret or worry. Instead of worrying, pray. Let petitions and praises shape your worries into prayers, letting God know your concerns.
Philippians 4:6 (MSG)

Rejoice always, pray continually, give thanks in all circumstances; for this is God's will for you in Christ Jesus.
1 Thessalonians 5:16-18 (NIV)

Each morning let me learn more about your love because I trust you. I come to you in prayer, asking for your guidance.
Psalm 143:8 (CEV)

We communicate with God through prayer. It has the power to change our situation and our daily atmosphere. When we direct our words to God, He leads us and reveals Himself to us in a deeper way.

———————

1. Are you taking the time to talk to God daily? If not, ask God to reveal to you the distractions in your life that keep you from doing so.

2. Prayer changes our attitude and perspective. In what areas of your life do you hold on to negativity? Pray through this and ask God to change your perspective.

3. Spend the next 15 minutes praying and asking God to reveal Himself to you. Write down the things that He places on your heart.

— 2 —
GOD'S WORD

God, forgive me for the times I set your Word aside and try to do life without it.

Dear God,

Thank you so much for giving me your written Word. I am so blessed to have access to knowledge about who You are, Your love for me, and how that love is displayed through the Gospel message. It is so uplifting to see Your faithfulness to Your people and to study Your redemptive plan throughout history. I'm deeply encouraged when I read accounts of people who, like myself, have also made mistakes and turned away from You. But what stirs my heart even more is reading through Your unending display of grace, love, and mercy upon Your children.

Despite my gratitude for your Word, I still find myself neglecting the blessing You put before me. God, forgive me for the days I set your Word aside and try to do life without it. My actions and emotions evidence the days that I am not resting in your truth. Teach me discipline to hide Your Word in my heart daily and to meditate on it day and night. Please give me an unquenchable thirst for it. May my desire to grow in knowledge of You come from a place of humility and not a heart seeking to puff itself up with pride.

Forgive me during times of trial when I immediately turn to others before even seeking guidance from Your Word. No book, preacher, spouse, blogger, or friend has the power that Your words alone have. Scripture should be my instinctive go-to. May it become my lifeline in all circumstances. As I navigate through trials, may it be a compass that points me back to what I know to be true about You.

God, may Your Word teach me discernment. In a technology-filled world, where headlines and news feeds are constantly in view, it is vital that the things entering my heart and mind go through a biblical filter. I want to be like the Bereans we read about in Thessalonians, weighing words against Scripture to ensure that what enters my ears lines up with what You have to say. May nothing be added to Your Word and nothing taken away.

Lord, You know my heart and my thoughts. If I'm being honest, I have to say that it can sometimes be intimidating when I approach Your Word. Thank You for sending the Holy Spirit as a guide to help me rightly interpret Scripture. Please reveal yourself to me as I navigate through it.

God, I ask that you open my heart and mind to be receptive to Your truth. Father, I am so blessed to have such a firm foundation to root myself in. When I anchor myself in Your Word alone, I find the security and peace that most spend a lifetime searching for, and for that I cannot thank you enough.

In Jesus's name I pray, amen.

So Jesus was saying to those Jews who had believed Him, "If you continue in My word, then you are truly disciples of Mine; and you will know the truth, and the truth will make you free."
John 8:31-32 (ESV)

All Scripture is breathed out by God and profitable for teaching, for reproof, for correction, and for training in righteousness, that the man of God may be competent, equipped for every good work.
2 Timothy 3:16-17 (ESV)

For the word of God is living and active, sharper than any two-edged sword, piercing to the division of soul and of spirit, of joints and of marrow, and discerning the thoughts and intentions of the heart.
Hebrews 4:12 (ESV)

The law of the Lord is perfect, reviving the soul; the testimony of the Lord is sure, making wise the simple; the precepts of the Lord are right, rejoicing the heart; the commandment of the Lord is pure, enlightening the eyes; the fear of the Lord is clean, enduring forever; the rules of the Lord are true, and righteous altogether. More to be desired are they than gold, even much fine gold; sweeter also than honey and drippings of the honeycomb. Moreover, by them is your servant warned; in keeping them there is great reward.
Psalm 19:7-11 (ESV)

The early morning hours are full of demands, ideas, and to-dos. Setting the pace and attitude of the day is established on the pages of God's word and our time spent with Him in prayer. His word is the sword that can cut any negative thoughts the enemy wants to use to distract us. Let us make it a priority to keep it on the tip of our tongues to recall at any moment of the day.

──────────────

1. Select Scripture this month to memorize and meditate on. Write it in your journal and somewhere you can see it every day.

2. Ask the Lord to make His word alive to you in a new way.

3. Pray that the Lord will give you an unquenchable thirst for the Word.

— 3 —

WORSHIP + GRATITUDE

Keep my eyes ever on You
& my heart will ever
praise You.

Father,

Too long my eyes have been downcast, my gaze set on what is small and utterly unimpressive. My sights have been set on me. But when I look at you? When I behold your beauty, your majesty? I am overwhelmed. I want to dwell in that sacred space, to build my nest in your holy rafters. In looking upon you, I am convinced that I will look upon your goodness in the land of the living, the land of the here and now. And I see it.

I see all the places where you have brought blessing in the midst of barrenness. I can begin to count up all the blessings: how you have healed my wounded heart, how you have redeemed my soul from pit-dwelling. And you didn't just leave me crusted with muck and mire, but you washed me whiter than snow and set a crown on my head. In loyal love and mercy, you have affectionately called me "daughter." You showed your steadfast love by sending your Son to live for me and to die for me. I cannot keep silent.

When I count the blessings, I can't help but give the thanks. My heart gushes through my lips in a song of praise. It may be my song or a song borrowed. Either way, it is heard and it is beautiful to you. The seeing, the counting, the thanking, the singing—it's all worship. Keep my eyes ever on you, and my heart will ever praise you.

One thing have I asked of the Lord, that will I seek after: that I may dwell in the house of the Lord all the days of my life, to gaze upon the beauty of the Lord and to inquire in his temple.

Psalm 27:4 (ESV)

I believe that I shall look upon the goodness of the Lord in the land of the living!

Psalm 27:13 (ESV)

Bless the Lord, O my soul, and forget not all his benefits, who forgives all your iniquity, who heals all your diseases, who redeems your life from the pit, who crowns you with steadfast love and mercy, who satisfies you with good so that your youth is renewed like the eagle's.

Psalm 103:2-5 (ESV)

Let them thank the Lord for his steadfast love for his wondrous works to the children of man!

Psalm 107:8, 15, 21, 31 (ESV)

Gratitude and worship are such sweet and beautiful love letters to our Lord. They acknowledge and praise His authorship, presence, and salvation in our lives. What a beautiful sight and music to His ears it must be to witness his children praising His name in speech and song.

———————————

1. Pour out on the page in drawing or words WHO God is to you.

2. Confess to the Lord any ways you have turned what are really blessings into complaints.

3. List 3 people in your life that you are thankful for and why. Then let them know in person, a phone call, or through a handwritten letter.

FAITH

Call us in our sleep,
call us when we wake,
flatten us before the throne
in the early hours of dawn.

Father,

What are you up to? It seems You are stirring the heavens again. Your wind whips the trees, Your moon turns red, and we gaze from the earth with our ear to the ground to listen.

We can't begin to fathom the work of Your hands. That's the way you intend it. We can't theorize or strategize, because You dwell in unexpectancy. You come out of left field, making the first last and the last first, and all You ask of us is what seems nearly impossible:

"Sell everything you have and follow me."
"Leave your father and mother and all you hold dear, and cling to me."
"Don't look to the right or the left, just fix your eyes on me."

I desperately want to, Father, but I am afraid. It feels too simple, too surrendered, and too free. You've proved yourself time and time again. Please remind me to keep trusting.

I want the curtain pulled back and the game plan revealed before I advance. But that is the very essence of faith, yes? Thank You for being the author and perfector of it, for if it were up to me, I'd keep checking my bank account and seeking to amass more temporal comforts. Please, Holy Father, keep me gazing toward the eternal.

I think of Joshua and how You repeatedly told him to be strong and courageous. I wish I could be like him, Lord. I want so desperately to be strong, yet You know how utterly weak I am.

So I ask You to fill me again. Fill each of us again. Consume Your holy people with a fire from heaven, and fix our feet on higher ground. Call us in our sleep, call us when we wake, flatten us on our face before your throne in the early hours of dawn.

May this posture ready us for the assignments You will give us. Have Your way in our hearts, Lord. Reveal Yourself in Your perfect time. In the meantime, steady our course and hold us close.

For all these things, we implore You in Jesus's name. You are Holy and righteous, and we count it unmerited favor to be called Your children. We are speechless that we will dwell in your house forevermore.

We are ever surrendered and ever grateful, amen.

Jesus answered, "If you want to be perfect, go, sell your possessions and give to the poor, and you will have treasure in heaven. Then come, follow me."
Matthew 19:21 (NIV)

That is why a man leaves his father and mother and is united to his wife, and they become one flesh.
Genesis 2:24 (NIV)

Do not turn to the right or the left; keep your foot from evil.
Proverbs 4:27 (NIV)

"So the last will be first, and the first will be last."
Matthew 20:16 (NIV)

"Be strong and very courageous. Be careful to obey all the law my servant Moses gave you; do not turn from it to the right or to the left, that you may be successful wherever you go. Keep this Book of the Law always on your lips; meditate on it day and night, so that you may be careful to do everything written in it. Then you will be prosperous and successful. Have I not commanded you? Be strong and courageous. Do not be afraid; do not be discouraged, for the LORD your God will be with you wherever you go."
Joshua 1:7-9 (NIV)

Our faith leads us in all areas of our daily life. It tells us where to go, what to do, and who to love on. Without our faith, all works are in vain. We must build up our faith to fully live out our mission and purpose. The beautiful thing about the gospel and sharing it is that there is no reason to overcomplicate it. No reason to follow a formula. Just share your story—the story of a God who saves and redeems.

————————

1. Do you truly trust God with your life? Full surrender and trust in the Lord is shown in how you make decisions, plan your days, and engage with people. Would others see that in your daily actions? Ask the Lord to build your faith right here in this moment. Is there anything He is laying on your heart? Write it down.

2. Are you designating time each day to seek God? Write down the ways you can pursue Him.

3. In what ways can you share your faith with others on a daily basis?

— 5 —

FREEDOM

Please show me your truth
So I may LOVE like you.

Dear Lord,

My heart's desire is to experience Your presence and to know You more. I ask you to prepare my heart to receive the fullness of the freedom Jesus paid for me at the cross. Holy Spirit, come and fill me with Your power and love.

I long to be still before You. Help me rest in Your presence and leave the distractions of my life at Your feet so I can climb in Your lap and abide. I want to be so close to You that I can hear Your thoughts regarding all the circumstances of my life. What do You want to talk to me about today?

I desire to be free from all the things that keep me entangled in busyness, sin, unforgiveness, or negative thought patterns. Unlock the areas in my life that are kept in bondage because of the deceit of the enemy. Show me where I need inner healing so I may rely on You as my only source for protection, comfort, and strength. Then I know I will be the person you created and redeemed me to be. May You be glorified in my life so that I may leave a legacy of grace, humility, faith, and mercy in Your honor.

Show me what lies I've been believing about myself, others, or You. I ask You to forgive me for believing those lies. Please show me your truth so I may love like You.

Reveal to me those I need to forgive so I may release them from all the consequences their actions have had in my life. I want to extend forgiveness in such a way that I can honestly say they owe me nothing. Please forgive me for carrying offense. I give to You those who have come to mind and ask that You abundantly bless them.

With Your help and guidance, I choose to break down any walls I've put up to protect myself that have kept me from my destiny. I choose to close any doors that have been opened by fear, hatred, sexual sin, or involvement with the ways of the enemy. I invite your presence, Jesus, and ask You to show me what has a hold on me so I may be in Your grip instead. I trust You to show me what I'm free to be now that those walls have come down and those doors have been shut.

I choose to cancel any agreements I've made, either knowingly or unknowingly, with what rejection, shame, anger, discouragement, perfectionism, busyness, jealousy, envy, strife, depression, or sexual immorality say about me or others. I repent of partnering with the enemy of my soul and ask that You come and heal those damaged places. Holy Spirit, reveal where I'm bound and create in me a pure heart and sound mind. Empower me to change the atmosphere wherever I go because You live in me.

I declare that I am set free from these things by the blood of the Lamb and the word of my testimony! Thank You, Lord, for Your forgiveness and grace. I worship You alone because You are worthy of all honor and praise. Thank You for my freedom, in Jesus's name!

Now the Lord is the Spirit, and where the Spirit of the Lord is, there is freedom.
2 Corinthians 3:17 (ESV)

For the weapons of our warfare are not of the flesh but have divine power to destroy strongholds. We destroy arguments and every lofty opinion raised against the knowledge of God, and take every thought captive to obey Christ.
2 Corinthians 10:4-5

For freedom Christ has set us free; stand firm therefore, and do not submit again to the yoke of slavery.
Galatians 5:1 (ESV)

And the effect of righteousness will be peace, and the result of righteousness, quietness and trust forever. My people will abide in a peaceful habitation, in secure dwellings, and in quiet resting places.
Isaiah 32:17-18 (ESV)

Free people free people. When we are not free and walking healed and whole, we make it very difficult for the Lord to use us as He desires. Oh, what beauty and abundant joy lies on the other side of freedom. So let's fight for freedom from bondage, from the lies of the enemy, from sin and unforgiveness.

———————————

1. List one area of your life the Lord wants you to find freedom in right now.

2. List one area of your life the Lord wants you to find healing in. Is there someone you need to forgive?

3. Ask the Lord to search your heart and reveal to you any sin in thought or action, and confess that before Him.

— 6 —
SEASONS

prepare my heart,
my mind and my spirit
for the unknown
Seasons ahead.

Father,

You are my hope and my resting place. In You alone I find peace and purpose. Your Word says there is a season for everything under the heavens. I pray that You would prepare my heart, my mind, and my spirit for the unknown seasons ahead. When I find myself in the seasons of life that are joyful and full of ease, I give You praise and thanksgiving because in those moments my soul is satisfied, and I am grateful.

In the days of drought, when I find myself seemingly alone in the wilderness and I wonder, "Will it all be okay?", give me the courage and strength to keep moving and to keep pushing. May Your presence overtake me and overwhelm me. When fear and doubt try to creep in, let me find Your hand gently holding mine. Let's walk this path together.

May I be intentional, fully present, and soak in every moment, because the days are fleeting. Lord, search my heart and know me. Give me eyes to see and ears to hear. Help me to rest in Your presence and stand on Your Word; to know You deeply and to be fully known by You. I want to praise You with reckless abandon regardless of my circumstances. Whether I'm in the valley or on the mountaintop, I pray You would pursue my heart and wrap Your loving arms around me. I need You. Give me a positive perspective and a renewed mind-set in each new season so that I may fully live out the mission You have called me to without distraction from the enemy. Encourage me to keep my eyes fixed on You. I pray You would continually find me faithful to Your Kingdom and to Your people. You are sovereign and good. In You, I am enough and can face the seasons ahead.

———————————

There is a time for everything, and a season for every activity under the heavens.
Ecclesiastes 3:1 (NIV)

Blessed are your eyes, because they see; and your ears, because they hear.
Matthew 13:16 (NIV)

Let us keep our eyes fixed on Jesus, on whom our faith depends from beginning to end.
Hebrews 12:2 (GNT)

Come to me, all you who are weary and burdened, and I will give you rest.
Matthew 11:28 (NIV)

We all experience different seasons in life. Some are challenging and full of growth, while others are abundant with joy and ease. Each new season is just as important as the last and contains opportunities to know God on a deeper level.

———————————

1. Would you describe your current life season as being in the valley or on the mountaintop?

2. What challenges have you encountered in this season? What joys have you experienced?

3. List all the ways God has provided for you in this season.

REST + BALANCE

You are the One that keeps me together

Heavenly Father,

When I feel tugged in every direction, center me back to You. When I feel overwhelmed, remind me that these roles You have trusted me with are a blessing and a privilege. When I am trying to do too many things at once, help me to focus on one thing at a time and strip away what I can do without. Help me not mistake busy with important, Lord, for unnecessary busy does not allow room for Your clarity. When I feel drained with all that's expected, rekindle my innocence of a time before so many things competed for my attention—the time of resolve in simple peace and quiet without the temptation of busy. Lord, show me balance.

When I am unraveling, You are the One who keeps me together. When I feel like I can't make time for rest, give me the security of knowing that You are my most fulfilling and gratifying investment. It is Your rest that renews my soul. Lord, help me not confuse rest with being unproductive. Your calm is the soft flicker of a flame so that I can be Your light and run with Your fire. Lord, give me rest.

When I want to control every detail, make me broken so You can make me whole. When I am hesitant, help me trust that You've brought me to this place in anticipation and excitement of doing Your will. When I am trying to force something, remind me that You have already written my story. When I feel weak, help me see these opportunities for those are the cracks

You're wanting to fill and the places You're wanting to grow. Lord, help me trust.

When I am tired and longing for balance, Lord, fill my everything with Your calm so I can rest in Your strength.

Hear my cry, O God; listen to my prayer. From the ends of the earth I call to you, I call as my heart grows faint; lead me to the rock that is higher than I. For you have been my refuge, a strong tower against the foe. I long to dwell in your tent forever and take refuge in the shelter of your wings.

Psalm 61:1 (NIV)

Do you not know? Have you not heard? The Lord is the everlasting God, the Creator of the ends of the earth. He will not grow tired or weary, and his understanding no one can fathom. He gives strength to the weary and increases the power of the weak. Even youths grow tired and weary, and young men stumble and fall; but those who hope in the Lord will renew their strength. They will soar on wings like eagles; they will run and not grow weary, they will walk and not be faint.

Isaiah 40:28- 31 (NIV)

"Come to me, all you who are weary and burdened, and I will give you rest. Take my yoke upon you and learn from me, for I am gentle and humble in heart, and you will find rest for your souls."

Matthew 11:28-30 (NIV)

Yes, my soul, find rest in God: my hope comes from him.

Psalm 62:5 (NIV)

When we are tired and weary, we cannot be all that we are created to be or do all that we are called to do. This is one reason God not only created but commanded the Sabbath. He calls us to work six days and then rest. Choosing to truly rest acknowledges that God is in control of everything, not us. It's saying, "I trust You enough to lay down the need to be productive today." Rest is not a luxury; it's obedience and surrender.

———————

1. Does resting make you feel guilty? If it does, confess the times you have forfeited the Sabbath in exchange for "being productive."

2. Ask the Lord to reveal people, activities, or situations that are keeping you from rest and balance.

3. Prayerfully list out the things that you need to do to maintain rest and balance in your life this month.

—— 8 ——

WELLNESS

From soul to skin,
I belong to you.

Dear Father,

Thank You that You are not confused, stressed, or anxious about me or Your plans for my life. You know the end from the beginning, and I can trust You with the things my finite mind cannot comprehend. For You have made me for yourself. From soul to skin, I belong to You. I belong to You to be put and kept together, holy and whole.

The world and all its expectations is "shoulding" on me. Man-made ideas of what I "should" do, who I "should" be, and even what I "should" look like when I do what I "should" do hoist a backpack of burdens upon me.

I confess that I easily lose focus, Father. I get distracted, stop listening for Your voice, and leave the door open for the spirit of anxiety and stress to come and steal my peace, health, whole-ness, and prosperity in You. In my anxiety and stress, I run to empty, broken places for false comfort: food, drink, exercise, and entertainment.

The pace of this world is getting faster, and I can't keep pace on its treadmill any more. I am jumping off. I want to hear Your voice saying, "Come this way." Lord, give me the strength to follow You wherever You are going. Wherever You go, at what-ever pace, is where my peace is found and I am made whole—heart, mind, soul, and strength.

You have set up all of creation to point me toward Your presence where I am made whole. On the days when my shoulders feel tight, my breath feels short, and my head pounds, may I be quick to notice these warning signs and run to You and not to my places of false comfort. Whisper to me the things You would have me do to combat the spirit of stress. I give You full permission to tell me what to eat, what to drink, what to think, when to work, when to play, and when to rest. Help me to care, like You care, for my whole life—my heart, my mind, my soul, and my body as an act of undying worship unto You, my King.

May God himself, the God who makes everything holy and whole, make you holy and whole, put you together - spirit, soul, and body - and keep you fit for the coming of our Master, Jesus Christ.
1 Thessalonians 5:23 (MSG)

Do not be anxious about anything, but in everything, by prayer and petition, with thanksgiving, present your requests to God. And the peace of God, which transcends all understanding, will guard your hearts and your minds in Christ Jesus.
Philippians 4:6-7 (NIV)

Do not conform any longer to the pattern of this world, but be transformed by the renewing of your mind. Then you will be able to test and approve what God's will is--his good, pleasing, and perfect will.
Romans 12:1-2 (NIV)

I heard a voice from heaven saying, "Write this: From now on those who die believing in the Lord are blessed." "Yes," says the Spirit. "Let them rest from their hard work. What they have done goes with them."
Revelation 14:13 (GWT)

How many times have our calling, purpose, or dreams been interrupted and even halted because we weren't feeling well? God cares deeply about our health and the level of stress we carry around every day. He didn't design us to carry the weight of the world. When we feel well, we can love well.

———————————

1. Praise the Lord for the areas of your life you have gained control of in managing your stress and health.

2. Ask the Lord to show you an area of your life that is causing unnecessary stress. Is it an activity, a person, your work, or even ministry?

3. List one change you can commit to make this month in regards to fitness, food, and fellowship that will improve your overall health.

9

AUTHENTICITY

Lord, help me to be real. To not hide the hard and only show/share the good.

Lord,

Some days I am just so weary. Weary of the expectations of this world to always have it all together. To have a perfect Instagram, clean home, and successful career. Some days I am so discouraged, as it looks like everyone else has a perfect life and I can't keep up with even one-third of mine. So often, Lord, it seems easier to put on a face and say "it's all good" when my heart feels the opposite. Instead, Lord God, help me to be real. To be vulnerable when appropriate. To not hide the hard and only show the good. Jesus, help me remember that we are jars of clay. We have cracks so that others can see YOU, FATHER, in us. So they can see Your peace when we endure trials, so they can see Your love when we are met with anger, so that others can see Your hope through our attitude in tough circumstances.

Lord, help me to seek who I am in You first. At the beginning of my day, those first moments of my day, help me tune my focus to the new creation I am in You. Guide my days to give You glory by being authentic. Help my interactions with others to be a refreshment and encouragement to their lives. Real, tough, joyful, challenging, and non-perfect is beautiful when I walk it step by step with You.

Gently remind my soul during those busy days where I get caught up in the world that You NEVER leave me. You are with me when I wake up and when I sit down. Even though I often forget, You are RIGHT there. Help me to continually seek You in all the moments of my day and seek Your will to share Your truth through the cracks of my everyday life. For when I seek You in my weakness, there is my true strength.

———————

But we have this treasure in jars of clay to show that this all-surpassing power is from God and not from us.
2 Corinthians 4:7 (NIV)

You know when I sit and when I rise; you perceive my thoughts from afar.
Psalm 139:2 (NIV)

That is why, for Christ's sake, I delight in weaknesses, in insults, in hardships, in persecutions, in difficulties. For when I am weak, then I am strong.
2 Corinthians 12:10 (NIV)

Be strong and courageous. Do not fear or be in dread of them, for it is the LORD your God who goes with you. He will not leave you or forsake you.
Deuteronomy 3:16 (ESV)

Living authentically is living a life reflective of who God says He is and what we believe about Him. We sometimes find ourselves wrestling somewhere between being too transparent and not transparent enough, between being our true self and striving to be a better version of who we are. So what does the Lord see as true authenticity and how do we live it out? God's word urges us to live a transparent life in community with others. He calls us to be authentic and genuine to ourselves and to those around us because there is freedom in truth. When we hide our true selves—the good, the bad, and the ugly—we are hindering ourselves from becoming the person God has called us to be.

———————

1. Is there any area of your life you are not living authentically (i.e., your true self)? Are you trying to be someone you aren't in order to receive approval from people?

2. Prayerfully consider how much to share publicly vs. privately. What needs to be reserved for you, the Lord, and your closest community?

3. Confess any ways you have misrepresented your true self and who you are when no one is looking.

10

IDENTITY

Therefore,
I take up
my right
to rebuke
the insecure life!

Heavenly Father,

You created the heavens and the earth with Your great power and outstretched arm. There is nothing too hard for You. Often times I fail to remember that You, this same God, created me with purpose in Your very image. In the middle of a modern-day society that conditions me to believe my value is found in what I do, what I know, who I know, and what I own, remind me that my value and my identity are simply found in You choosing to say "yes" to creating me.

You formed me, molded me, and carefully crafted every detail of my persona for your glory. Lord, it is through You that I have identity. The value of my life exists because of You. Thank You. Because of this, there is nothing I can do, right or wrong, to change who I am. There is no title, position, or possession that adds or subtracts to whose I am. In You, my worth is found.

Father, when I am tempted to believe anything that doesn't line up with this truth, help me destroy the destructive tapes that play in my mind. Encourage me to replace thoughts of self-doubt, insecurity, and self-destruction with God thoughts that mirror the truth of Your Word. Guide me to your promises that affirm me as a rightful heir in You.

When I struggle with the reflection I see in the mirror, remind me that Your hands carefully crafted my appearance, my features, and shape; to slander myself is to slander You. Father, You looked at the whole of my creation and called it very good. Please convict me when I call myself anything less.

Rescue me from making decisions for family, friends, my business, and myself that are rooted in any form of insecurity or fear. Wash over me the peace of knowing your perfect love casts out fear. Therefore, I take up my right to rebuke the insecure life. Affirm me in knowing that I was created to feel safe, secure, confident, and bold; it's part of my spiritual DNA as a born-again believer in Christ.

Heavenly Father, help me believe You when You say I am enough. Encourage me to apply the comfort of Your Word to the places in me sensitive to the effects of the world. Turn my eyes to Jesus, the author and finisher of my faith.

Lord, make me brave. Give me courage to rise as a daughter who finds every ounce of her value in You so that others will be inspired to rise to the same calling of confident identity.

God spoke: "Let us make human beings in our image, make the reflecting our nature So they can be responsible for the fish in the sea, the birds in the air, the cattle, and, yes, Earth itself, and every animal that moves on the face of Earth." God created human beings; he created them godlike, reflecting God's nature. He created them male and female. God looked over everything he had made; it was so good, so very good!
Genesis 1:26-27 & 31 (MSG)

No weapon forged against you will prevail, and you will refute every tongue that accuses you. This is the heritage of the servants of the Lord, and this is their vindication from me declares the Lord.
Isaiah 54:17 (NIV)

And I am convinced that nothing can ever separate us from God's love. Neither death nor life, neither angels nor demons, neither our fears for today nor our worries about tomorrow—not even the powers of hell can separate us from God's love. No power in the sky above or in the earth below—indeed, nothing in all creation will ever be able to separate us from the love of God that is revealed in Christ Jesus our Lord."
Romans 8:38-39 (NLT)

Even as [in His love] He chose us [actually picked us out for Himself as His own] in Christ before the foundation of the world, that we should be holy (consecrated and set apart for Him) and blameless in His sight, even above reproach, before Him in love. For He foreordained us (destined us, planned in love for us) to be adopted (revealed) as His own children through Jesus Christ, in accordance with the purpose of His will [because it pleased Him and was His kind intent]
Ephesians 1:4-5 (AMP)

In today's society, we are told that our value and worth are found in our career, how much money we make, and what we look like. If we listen to society, we develop a poor self-image, doubt our purpose, and never feel good enough. But our true identity is found in Christ alone.

———————————

1. Write a list of all the ways you have allowed society to dictate your self-worth. Pray through this list and ask God to give you freedom and clarity in each area.

2. What are your strengths and God-given gifts? If you're not sure, ask God to reveal them to you.

3. When we serve others, we take the focus off ourselves and our own insecurities. In what ways can you serve those around you?

11

GRACE IN MY HOME

i need help
Choosing grace in
my home

Lord,

You told me in your Word to come to you with my every care and burden. Here I am. I am here because I need help choosing grace in my home.

What a gift it would be to have a home seasoned with the grace You freely give and that, in some small way, all who come in would feel it. I pray You would help me find a balance in keeping a lovely dwelling for those who are within these walls without becoming consumed with flawlessness. Who I truly am will show itself under this roof, so please retell this heart of mine the story of Your grace and how it can be found in my mistakes and faults. Help me to then walk in it and that it would be woven in the interactions I have with others. An ebb and flow of grace being received and given back out—what a beautiful home that would be.

At the end of the day when I lay my head on my pillow, I want to rest because of You. Keep me from lying awake recounting all my failures for the day with a heavy chest of defeat. Keep me from finding peace in my own works if I happened to have a smooth day. My desire is to rest my head with a humble spirit knowing full well all my successes are because of You and all my failures are covered in Your grace because of Christ.

...casting all your anxiety on Him, because He cares for you.
1 Peter 5:7 (NIV)

Let us then with confidence draw near to the throne of grace, that we may receive mercy and find grace to help in time of need.
Hebrews 4:16 (ESV)

...he saved us, not because of righteous things we had done, but because of his mercy. He saved us through the washing of rebirth and renewal by the Holy Spirit, whom he poured out on us generously through Jesus Christ our Savior, so that, having been justified by his grace, we might become heirs having the hope of eternal life. This is a trustworthy saying. And I want you to stress these things, so that those who have trusted in God may be careful to devote themselves to doing what is good. These things are excellent and profitable for everyone
Titus 3: 5-8 (NIV)

...for we are his workmanship, created in Christ Jesus for good works, which God prepared beforehand, that we should walk in them.
Ephesians 2:10 (ESV)

Our home is the place where grace is required every day with our spouse, our children, our friends, and ourselves. Our pursuit of perfection can become the thing that takes back control from God and says, "I don't need You." Not extending grace to others dismisses the very sacrifice Christ made on the cross for you and me.

———————

1. Ask the Lord to show you some areas within your family and friends where you have not shown grace recently. Confess to the Lord and your family and ask forgiveness.

2. Write out the tangible ways the Lord has shown His grace in your life this month.

3. Is grace something you struggle with extending to yourself? In what areas of your personal life do you need to cut yourself a break?

—— 12 ——
SIMPLICITY

Jesus, I pray you'll help me quiet my home so my focus doesn't stray.

Dear Jesus,

Before I take another breath, I want to pause and say thank you for all the blessings and tangible gifts you've given me. Thank you for not only promising to always take care of me but for helping me to see that you are *indeed* always taking care of me. Thank you for my family and our commitment to support one another continuously in health and sickness, when we have much and when we have little.

Lord, I have a desire to put my family and our dreams—the dreams you've placed in our hearts—before the worldly things we own. There are days when my eyes wander and jealous feelings saturate my mind. I compare myself and my possessions to neighbors and strangers, and I admit I allow the things they own to take priority in my mind over my focus on You. Lord, help me to remember that keeping You at the forefront of my life pleases You. Help me to remember that our worldly possessions aren't to become idols. Help me keep my eyes focused on You and the dreams You've given me.

Help me to remember that when you bless us with tangible gifts, we are to receive them with open hands. It's not wrong to have "things," but it is wrong to place these "things" above You. Help me to learn how to live with less so that I can be filled with the riches of heaven.

I often crave simplicity, but sometimes I struggle with what that looks like. Lord, open my eyes and show me.

And while my heart desires quiet time with you, it's so easy for the noise of the world to overthrow my intentions. Jesus, I pray You'll help me quiet my home so my focus doesn't stray. Help me to cherish what You've blessed me with so my heart doesn't fill with greed or jealousy.

———————

Yet true godliness with contentment is itself great wealth. After all, we brought nothing with us when we came into the world, and we can't take anything with us when we leave it. So if we have enough food and cloth-ing, let us be content.
1 Timothy 6:6-8 (NLT)

So I concluded there is nothing better than to be happy and enjoy ourselves as long as we can. And people should eat and drink and enjoy the fruits of their labor, for these are gifts from God. And I know that whatever God does is final. Nothing can be added to it or taken from it. God's purpose is that people should fear him.
Ecclesiastes 3:12-14 (NLT)

But let me say this, dear brothers and sisters: The time that remains is very short. So from now on, those with wives should not focus only on their marriage. Those who weep or who rejoice or who buy things should not be absorbed by their weeping or their joy or their possessions. Those who use the things of the world should not become attached to them. For

this world as we know it will soon pass away.
1 Corinthians 7:29-31 (NLT)

Do not love this world nor the things it offers you, for when you love the world, you do not have the love of the Father in you. For the world offers only a craving for physical pleasure, a craving for everything we see, and pride in our achievements and possessions. These are not from the Father, but are from this world. And this world is fading away, along with everything that people crave. But anyone who does what pleases God will live forever.
1 John 2:15-17 (NLT)

Simple living isn't just about freeing up space in our homes; it's about freeing up time, resources, and even energy. Every day, we spend energy managing material things, schedules, and people. Living with less clears the clutter so we can live a life reflective of what really matters.

———————————

1. Ask the Lord what living simply looks like for you and your family.

2. Choose one area of your life that needs some clutter cleared this month and ask the Lord to reveal some action steps. Here are some ideas: stuff, schedule, distractions, people, activities...

3. Describe how you feel when clutter is cleared, space is found, and energy is renewed in your physical, mental, and emotional life.

—— 13 ——
SERVING

Lord,
   Help me
believe that
I can make
a difference.

Lord,

Give me Your eyes for the people and the needs around me. Give me Your heart for Your children and for serving them. Help me to act justly, to love mercy, and to walk humbly with you. I want to stand up for justice for people in my neighborhood and on the other side of the globe. I want to find the balance between justice and mercy, keeping a soft heart along the way. Most of all, I want to do it all for Your glory and Your kingdom...not mine.

Help me to have the courage to use my gifts and talents to serve. Help me to truly believe that no skill or talent or fire in my heart is too small for You to use. Put a cause on my heart, Lord. Someone to serve or something to fight for. Help me to find the balance between using all that I have and all that I am to fight for that cause and the responsibility I have to my family and business. Help me to set boundaries for giving that honor both you and my time, family, and business.

Lord, help me believe that I can make a difference. That serving and giving doesn't always mean moving to Africa but that there are plenty of ways to serve in my everyday life. Help me to not overthink what I need to do or how I need to do it, but rather help me to be bold enough to just begin Your work. I know that You can use me in big ways for big things. God, I want to believe that I can make a difference.

He has showed you, O man, what is good. And what does the LORD require of you? To act justly and to love mercy and to walk humbly with your God.

Micah 6:8 (NIV)

Do not merely listen to the word, and so deceive yourselves. Do what it says.

James 1:22 (ESV)

Just as each of us has one body with many members, and these members do not all have the same function, so in Christ we who are many form one body, and each member belongs to all the others. We have different gifts, according to the grace given us. If a man's gift is prophesying, let him use it in proportion to his faith. If it is serving, let him serve; if it is teaching, let him teach; if it is encouraging, let him encourage; if it is contributing to the needs of others, let him give generously; if it is leadership, let him govern diligently; if it is showing mercy, let him do it cheerfully.

Romans 12:4-8 (NIV)

...and if you spend yourselves in behalf of the hungry and satisfy the needs of the oppressed, then your light will rise in the darkness, and your night will become like the noonday.

Isaiah 58:10 (NIV)

For many of us, our acts of service will not look like Africa; it will look like our families and our neighborhoods. May we never minimize or compare how God is calling us to serve or how he has burdened our hearts to anyone else's burden or calling. And may we never neglect the power of how one person can impact the global needs of our world.

————————

1. Are you confident and secure in the area God has called you to serve right now in your life? If not, pray for clarity.

2. Are you maintaining a healthy balance between serving and giving and not compromising your own health or the health of your family? Confess where it has been out of balance and ask the Lord for clarity.

3. Lift up in prayer one immediate need around you and one global need in the world that God is calling you to focus on during this season of your life.

—— 14 ——
LOVING {WELL}

Sweet Lord —
Use my hands, use my
heart, use my ability
to love others well
because you first loved us.

Sweet Father,

Thank You for how You love us completely. How great and magnificent and powerful and lasting Your love is and always promises to be. You are the giver of life and the hope of things to come. You have called us to love Your people and by Your grace, I pray that we will walk in that calling today and each day to come.

I pray that You would open my eyes to the calling You have set before me and that I would act on that calling, relentlessly and without fear, to love others. I pray that You would creatively inspire, challenge, and pursue me daily to step out of my comfort zone, so that I could share my time, my words, my encouragement, and my love with others. Use me, Lord; use my hands, use my heart, use my ability to love others well because You first loved us.

Father, I pray that You would release me from my agenda, my plans, and my hopes for my life. Instead, I pray that You would radically open me up to Your plans, Your hopes, and Your kingdom to come. Use me, use all of us, to be a part of Your greater story. Father, use our homes to invite others in, to sit around our tables for times of shared meals, fellowship, and community. Use our hearts to come together in loving hope, to rest, listen, and be the body of Christ for one another. Use our hands and give me words and encouragement to send notes and letters of affirmation to others. Show me who needs love. Use our minds and give us discernment and wisdom to speak truth into each other's lives.

Father, I pray that You would discipline us to make the time to serve one another in love. To break away from our busy schedules and our to-do lists; instead, allow us to be reset by Your agenda, for Your people, because of Your heart for this broken world. May I never be too busy to love and see those in need of love around me. Use each of us to be your hands and feet here in our own homes, in our own communities, in our own cities.

To love others.
To serve others.
To engage with others.
To pursue others.

Give me the eyes to see and the heart to love. Fill me up with Your grace, Your abounding presence, and Your unending love, and send me out to do Your will today: to love others well. affirmation to others. Show me who needs love. And use our minds and give us discernment and wisdom to speak truth into each other's lives.

But it was because the Lord loved you and kept the oath he swore to your ancestors that he brought you out with a mighty hand and redeemed you from the land of slavery, from the power of Pharaoh king of Egypt. Know therefore that the Lord your God is God; he is the faithful God, keeping his covenant of love to a thousand generations of those who love him and keep his commandments.
Deuteronomy 7: 8-9 (NIV)

"I will give you a new heart and put a new spirit in you; I will remove from you your heart of stone and give you a heart of flesh. And I will put my Spirit in you and move you to follow my decrees and be careful to keep my laws. Then you will live in the land I gave your ancestors; you will be my people, and I will be your God."
Ezekiel 36: 26-28 (NIV)

"A new command I give you: Love one another. As I have loved you, so you must love one another. By this everyone will know that you are my disciples, if you love one another."
John 13: 34-35 (NIV)

For God so loved the world that he gave his one and only Son, that whoever believes in him shall not perish but have eternal life.
John 3:16 (NIV)

God's Word constantly encourages us and urges us to love and serve others. Jesus was our greatest example of servanthood. Our greatest calling is to love and serve others like Jesus did, but in the hustle and bustle of life, we tend to forget this great calling. Let's be intentional to create the time and space in our lives to pour into others.

———————

1. In what ways can you serve your friends and neighbors? Be creative and specific.

2. Are there any people in your life that you need to ask for their forgiveness? Ask God to reveal them to you and lay on your heart any actions you need to take.

3. Who are the top 5 people in your life that build you up? List all the ways you can pour into their lives on a continual basis.

—— 15a ——
SINGLENESS

now is the only
now I have
with You in
complete devotion
& focus

Jesus,

I want more of You. I need more of You. I crave more of You. Sometimes it's easy for me to forget that. I often get caught up in the wishing and longing for what I don't have that I forget You. Your arms are outstretched waiting for me, but I'm not even looking at You. Jesus, remind me to look at You. I want to gaze upon Your beauty. I want to be enthralled with You, the pursuer of my heart. I want to see You rightly.

Thank You for the desires and dreams you have placed inside of me. I thank You for the man that You have planned just for me. I look forward to the dreams we will have together. I know that he will believe in me, support me, challenge me, encourage me, and propel me into my destiny. Ultimately, I know we will point each other closer to You. I trust that Your watch is set to the perfect time and that my husband will come when You send him. Help me not to waste my time worrying about the details that You've already planned.

Right now, help me to lock eyes with You, the lover of my soul. Now is the only now I have with You in complete devotion and focus. I don't want to waste a second of it. I don't want to miss what You have for me in this season. Help me to embrace You above all. Help me to take more time with You, to press in deeper, to love harder. Help me to choose to run into Your arms instead of to things that don't matter. Thank You for using my business and whatever I put my hands to, to glorify You.

You will always be my first love. You will always be my true love. You can truly satisfy me.

————————

Her aim is to be devoted to the Lord in both body and spirit.
1 Corinthians 7:34a (NIV)

Oh true God, You are my God, the One in whom I trust. I seek You with every fiber of my being.
Psalm 63:1a (VOICE)

My soul clings to You; Your right hand reaches down and holds me up.
Psalm 63:8 (VOICE)

As the Father has loved me, so have I loved you. Abide in my love.
John 15:9 (ESV)

We have all experienced being single at one time or another, but do we always see the value in it? So often, especially as women, we feel that if we are single, we are missing out on something and that our lives are incomplete. Continue to pray boldly with open hands for God's perfect will while remaining available for everything He desires to accomplish during this season of singleness. You will not want to miss out on what He has in store.

———————

1. Do you find yourself wasting time and worrying about the details of your life that haven't happened yet? Write a prayer to God asking for a renewed and refocused mind-set.

2. Do you trust that God will sustain you and that He is enough?

3. What opportunities do you have in this season of singleness that will allow you to draw closer to God and His people? Praise God for those opportunities.

—— 15b ——
MARRIAGE

Lord, come – right in the
middle of our
marriage
ignite our hearts with
love for You

FOR SPIRITUAL UNITY

Father God, I lift up my marriage to You. Thank You that You are a shield around us, a covering from anything that could be distracting or destructive to the oneness You intend for us.

As You surround us, Lord, would You also come right in the middle of our relationship and ignite our hearts with a fresh love for You and for each other? Let the heat of Your presence be what binds us, connects us, and unifies us.

FOR WISE WORDS

Lord, as Creator, You spoke and the world came into being. As Savior, You spoke and the sick were healed. As a wife, help me to harness the surging power of my words.

I pray for my tongue to be under the control of the Holy Spirit, that I would use my words to build up my husband and our marriage, never to tear it down. When we're hanging with friends, just us in the privacy of our home, or when I'm out for work meetings, help me to use every opportunity to honor him with my words.

FOR HUMBLE LOVE

Lord, when the day comes to an end and my mind is reeling with business ideas and to-do lists, I need Your help shifting gears from me to "we." It's easy to be consumed with my projects, my vision, my needs. I ask for listening ears to your Spirit, that You would teach me how to look out for his needs above my own. Give me the grace to be a good listener, a wise encourager, and a safe place where he feels respected, affirmed, and cared for.

FOR MIND-BLOWING SEX

Lord, I'm grateful for the emotional, physical, and spiritual connection that sex brings. I thank You for my husband's sex drive and for the privilege of being his wife—the only one who can meet this very real need of his. At the end of those long days when I'm tired and not "in the mood," I pray for grace to choose connection and oneness and for the energy to bless my husband and be blessed by his love.

I pray that we would enjoy sex as You created it to be enjoyed. I ask that the joy we experience together would be more than we can ask for or imagine because of the ways You are working in our midst. I ask that our intimate relationship be cloaked in selfless love, connection, and mind-blowing pleasure. Where we need healing, Lord, heal. Where we've become complacent, Lord, stir us again, that we would serve and bless each other with this precious gift of physical intimacy.

In all things, Lord, I pray that You would unify our hearts, minds, and bodies, that we would be one in worship, one in love, and one in mission. In the mighty name of Jesus, amen.

For you bless the godly, O LORD; you surround them with your shield of love.
Psalm 5:12 (NLT)

A wise woman builds her home, but a foolish woman tears it down with her own hands.
Proverbs 14:1 (NLT)

Then make my joy complete by being like-minded, having the same love, being one in spirit and of one mind. Do nothing out of selfish ambition or vain conceit. Rather, in humility value others above yourselves, not looking to your own interests but each of you to the interests of the others.
Philippians 2:2-4 (NIV)

God can do anything, you know—far more than you could ever imagine or guess or request in your wildest dreams! He does it not by pushing us around but by working within us, his Spirit deeply and gently within us.
Ephesians 3:20 (MSG)

Marriage is a covenant created by God. In marriage, we go through different seasons—some easy and some hard—but the common ground should always be our faith in God and trust in each other. Marriage is made up of commitment, faith, emotions, and physical oneness. It takes intentionality to make sure each area is tended to and strengthened.

———————

1. Prayer is one of the most important things in marriage. It brings unity and clarity of mind as we seek God individually and with our spouse. What areas of your marriage need to be strengthened by God, and in what areas do you need to surrender?

2. Words should be used to build up, not to tear down. In what ways can you build up your spouse with your words?

3. Sex may be an area of insecurity and frustration in many marriages, but God intended intimacy to be a joyful experience. When it comes to sex in your marriage, are there any areas you need freedom in order to fully give yourself to each other?

— 16 —
MOTHERHOOD

Let my words be gracious and tender, let my actions be worthy of copying. Help me to be always slow to react and quick to forgive

Dear Heavenly Father,

Oh, I love you. Thank you for loving me so much and for having a heart for me. You are good. Thank you for entrusting me with the most precious gifts in the world: these tiny souls that you have me loving and teaching and serving. My little heartbeats! God, I beg of you, help me trust you with them. Give me open hands. Lord, remind me that you love them even more than I do. Help me daily as I set an example for them. Let my words be gracious and tender, let my actions be worthy of copying, help me to be always slow to react and quick to forgive. Let me show them what grace and love are on a daily basis.

God, you created me for a purpose. You gave me gifts and talents and dreams and passions and have me here for a specific reason. I pray in the name of Jesus Christ, who shed His blood for me, against guilt that is not from You. Guilt that comes with being a dreamer and a doer and a mama. God, show me that I am being an example to my little ones as a woman who is leaning on You, waiting on You to reveal Your calling and purpose in my life and then pursuing those dreams in line with what that calling and purpose is. Jesus, help me run full speed toward those dreams. Those are from You. You placed them in my heart for a reason. Don't let doubts and whispers slow me down. I pray against the fear and the doubts that sneak in, Lord.

God, I pray that I will not let my sweet babies become my idols. I don't want my role as a mama, as important as it is, to get in the way of what my job here on earth is for You. Remind me that both can be done well. Remind me that I can be an amazing mama while I walk in Your purpose for my life, whatever that looks like. God, help me lay down the fears that come with motherhood. The fears of open hands with my most precious gifts. The guilt and worry that I am not enough. The doubt that I cannot do it all. God, you made me, you know me, you love me. Jesus, keep my eyes fixed on You, and I trust that the rest will fall into place.

———————

Let your light shine before men, that they may see your good deeds and praise your Father in heaven.
Matthew 5:16 (NASB)

You are salt of the earth... you are the light of the world.
Matthew 5:13-14 (NIV)

I can do all things through Him who strengthens me.
Philippians 4:11 (NASB)

God made us. He created us to belong to Christ Jesus. Now we can do good things. Long ago God prepared them for us to do.
Ephesians 2:10 (NIRV)

Motherhood can be tiresome. It's the never-ending job that doesn't allow for vacation or sick days. It can be easy to disengage from our children due to pure exhaustion, and if we are not careful, we can allow "mom guilt" to overtake us. But let's take a moment to change our perspective. Our children need us fully present in their lives—free of distraction, guilt, and fear. When we rely on God, He is faithful to give us strength and change our attitude.

———————

1. Are there any distractions or time-wasters that are interfering with the time you spend with your children? (e.g., social media, TV, household chores)

2. List a few examples of how you can show your children grace and love when things aren't going according to plan. Then, list all the ways God has blessed you in motherhood.

3. When we make time for ourselves, we can better serve our family. It's important to have "me" time to feel refreshed and refocused. List a few ways you can treat yourself in order to recharge for your family. (e.g., coffee date, journaling, hot bath)

— 17 —
DREAMS

Today, Lord, I open my palms
before you and hold up all my
dreams. I spread open my fingers
Allow any dreams that are not
from you to fall to the ground, unplanted.

Dear Lord,

For as long as I can remember, I've had many dreams. To have a family and to make a difference in this world. To create. My mind takes me back to memories and moments when the seed-dreams were planted, yet through the years my dreams often became bigger than You. It was easy to chase after my little dreams, especially when Your big dreams cost so much. Today I pray that I will waste no more time on my good ideas. I pray, Lord, that Your dreams will be the center of my heart's pursuit.

Today, Lord, I open my palms before You and hold up all my dreams. I spread open my fingers. Allow any dreams that are not from You to fall to the ground unplanted. I relinquish all the dreams that are not Your dreams for me. Help me, Lord, to fix my gaze on Your perfect dreams for me. Let me not turn back.

I know that You love me completely. I know that You have my ultimate good in mind. I know that, in the end, the dreams You choose for me are good and best … even though they will mean other dreams fall to the wayside. I trust You, Lord, and I pray that I may trustYou more. Help me to choose what You choose with a glad heart.

Finally, I pray, Lord, that I will not compare my dreams to others. I pray that You will give me the strength to what You called me alone to do. I pray that my family and friends, neighbors and

watchers, will see You through me and in me. And for every dream that blooms and brings a harvest, may You get the glory. Amen.

———————

"For I know the plans I have for you," declares the LORD, "plans to prosper you and not to harm you, plans to give you hope and a future.
Jeremiah 29:11 (NLT)

But the LORD's plans stand firm forever; his intentions can never be shaken.
Psalm 33:11 (NLT)

How precious to me are your thoughts, God! How vast is the sum of them!
Psalm 139:17 (NLT)

Many plans are in a man's heart, But the counsel of the LORD will stand.
Proverbs 19:21 (NASB)

As dreamers and doers, we are always creating, thinking, and pursuing. It's important to keep God at the center of our doings and to allow our faith to lead us, giving every dream and idea to the Lord and asking what He wants us to pursue.

1. List the dreams and ideas you have that need inspiration and guidance from God. Then, pray through them.

2. Are there any dreams that you need to let go of? If you're not sure, ask God to show you.

3. Is there anything in your life distracting you or holding you back from going after your dreams or executing your ideas? Ask the Lord for help.

MY SPOUSE'S DREAMS

Lord, give him a heart to love you first, and to be fully devoted to his family.

Dear Lord,

I want to thank You for loving me unconditionally and consistently in spite of my inconsistencies and failures. But most of all, I want to thank You for my family and for my husband who was prepared and created just for me.

Lord, how I thank You.

Lord, how I thank you that my husband has a heart to chase and serve You. Lord, give him a heart to love You first and be fully devoted to his family. Lord, I ask that You continue to bless my husband in every area of his life, as he has been tasked with being a protector, provider, and prophet for our family.

Father, as I think about how my husband loves me unconditionally, thank you for the times he supports me in my dream-chasing endeavors, I ask that You remember him and those things that You have called him to do!

Bless the hands of his works and grant unto him the supernatural favor of God! Cover him with Your blood and let no weapon formed against him prosper. Send Your angelic host before him to clear his daily pathway. Let his steps be ordered by You, and grant unto him an unquenchable thirst to continue to seek You and Your ways.

Father, I ask that as he continues to chase You that You would grant unto him those things that his heart desires concerning his purpose and destiny. I ask that You will remove all obstacles, distractions, and hindrances that may be a threat to his purpose and his destiny.

Father, I ask that where he does not have clarity in his calling and purpose, that You would give him clarity.

Father, allow me to be the wife and helpmate that You have called me to be, one who would be strategic in prayer and one who would be of grace, integrity, and wise in counsel to her husband. Lord, allow me to encourage him when the days seem hazy; allow me to be the wind beneath his wings to hold him up when he becomes weak. Father, allow me to be a wife who would champion her husband with Your patience and unconditional love.

Give my husband confidence, boldness, zeal, and every resource needed to carry out the assignment that You have called him to do that will bring glory and honor to Your name and a smile to Your heart!

No weapon that is formed against thee shall prosper; and every tongue that shall rise against thee in judgment thou shalt condemn. This is the heritage of the servants of the LORD, and their righteousness is of me, saith the LORD.
Isaiah 54:17 (KJV)

Delight yourself in the LORD; And He will give you the desires of your heart.
Psalm 37:4 (NASB)

A wife of noble character who can find? She is worth far more than rubies. Her husband has full confidence in her and lacks nothing of value. She brings him good, not harm, all the days of her life.
Proverbs 31:10-12 (NIV)

She speaks with wisdom, and faithful instruction is on her tongue. She watches over the affairs of her household and does not eat the bread of idleness. Her children arise and call her blessed; her husband also, and he praises her.
Proverbs 31: 26-28 (NIV)

Having a spouse is a blessing that we can easily take for granted if we are not careful. Our spouse's dreams are just as important as our own personal dreams, and we must take the time to pour into them and encourage them on a daily basis.

———————————

1. Instead of directly nagging your spouse, go to God first and lift him up. In what ways do you need to pray for your spouse specifically?

2. Your spouse needs to know you support him and his dreams. How can you celebrate your spouse daily and show him your support?

3. In what ways has your spouse supported you? List all the ways you have been blessed by your spouse. Let's live in a state of gratitude toward him!

—18b—
MY CHILDREN'S DREAMS

Lord, give them dreams that are bigger than themselves, and Lord give them the Faith to fuel their dreams unto manifestation.

Dear Lord,

Heavenly Father, you have blessed us with the joy and care of our children. Give us strength, patience, and wisdom as we bring them up in your word, that we may teach them to love whatever is just and true and good, following the example of You, our Lord and Savior Jesus Christ.

I thank You, Father, that Your Word prevails over our children.

Lord, I am so glad that You know our children. Thank You for sending a hedge of angels around each of them. Thank You for protecting them daily. Father, incline their ears and turn their minds and hearts toward You and pleasing You as they seek their dreams.

Lord, give them dreams that are bigger than themselves—and, Lord, give them the faith to fuel their dreams into manifestation. Give them a will and heart to be all You created them to be. Help them to work hard and be successful. Enable them to be generous to those who are less fortunate. Give them hearts full of love and compassion for others.

You have told us that without vision, we perish. So, Father in heaven, knowing that, we can ask You to deposit in their minds and hearts of that particular dream, the special vision You have for their lives.

Along with their dreams, You will give them whatever graces, patience, and endurance it takes to see their dreams through.

My prayer is that they chase and aspire to live a life that would please You. I pray that they would seek You with their whole heart. Father, most of all I pray that as they seek You. I ask that You would order their steps in their journey to pursue their dreams and You would open copious doors of possibilities filled with opportunities.

My prayer is that You would enlarge their territory, expand their tent, and grant increase in every area of their lives as they pursue their dreams. Father, I decree and declare that there will not be any delays, denials, nor setbacks as they pursue their dreams, and that they shall live a life full of promise, success, and victory!

———————

"For I know the plans I have for you," declares the Lord, "plans to prosper you and not to harm you, plans to give you hope and a future."
Jeremiah 29:11 (NIV)

So the word of the Lord continued to increase and prevail mightily.
Acts 19:20 (ESV)

For the LORD gives wisdom; from his mouth come knowledge and understanding.
Proverbs 2:6 (NIV)

The dreams and aspirations of our children are a beautiful thing, especially when they are God-inspired. As parents, let's make it a point to encourage and celebrate the creativity in our children.

————————

1. List the ways you can specifically pray for your child and his or her dreams.

2. How can you encourage your child on a daily basis to show your support?

3. Children follow our example, so it's important for them to see us ambitious as well. What activities can you do together to help spark their creativity?

—— 19 ——
FEARS

I will NOT let
FEAR take
ahold of me and
stop me from what
I know you are
calling me to do.

Oh Lord,

You are with me. I will not be afraid.

I need You, Lord. I cannot do anything alone. I step out. One foot in front of each other. I don't see the outcome, and that terrifies me. I want to always know what's next, but I choose instead to trust You. I will not let fear take a hold of me and stop me from what I know You are calling me to do.

Why do I ever doubt? You always meet me and guide me to where you are taking me. You always open the doors You want me to walk through and close the doors You want me to walk away from.

Give me strength to obey what You ask of me, for it is obedience that pleases You.

God, You are great and mighty. You see all and know all. I don't know why I ever let my worries bring me down. I let them turn circles in my head when I know that does nothing but cause me more fear. Why do I worry when I can instead pray?

I bring these thoughts before You and surrender them. As storms surround me, I draw close to You and ask that You bring Your peace that passes all understanding to my soul. Let not my heart be troubled, let me not be afraid. Show me that You are with me. Let me feel Your presence as I make decisions each day. You know me better than I know myself. You see what's ahead of me, and I know that I can trust You. May Your truth ring in my ears as I walk forward in boldness and put my confident trust in you. Amen.

———————

Do not be anxious about anything, but in everything by prayer and supplication with thanksgiving let your requests be made known to God. And the peace of God, which surpasses all understanding, will guard your hearts and your minds in Christ Jesus.
Philippians 4:6-7 (ESV)

The LORD is with me; I will not be afraid. What can man do to me?
Psalm 118:6 (ESV)

So do not fear, for I am with you; do not be dismayed, for I am your God. I will strengthen you and help you; I will uphold you with my righteous right hand.
Isaiah 41:10 (ESV)

Peace I leave with you; my peace I give to you. Not as the world gives do I give to you. Let not your hearts be troubled, neither let them be afraid.
John 14:27 (ESV)

The enemy's favorite weapon in our world today is fear. He uses it in such cunning ways to make us believe God is not in control. But we have the upper hand through Christ because where fear resides, our faith can rise. We serve a mighty God who sits on His throne and fights on our behalf against the enemy every second of every day.

————————

1. What fear have you overcome in the last 3 months? Give praise and thanks to the Lord for finding freedom from that fear!

2. Confess an area of your life right now where fear is paralyzing you. Write out all the worst-case scenarios and counter them with Scripture that reveals that God can and will still be in control.

3. Describe what your fear looks and feels like. Write out 3 action steps to take when you see that fear taking hold of your spirit. Some examples might be: Scripture, a prayer, a word, or calling a friend.

COMPARISON

keep me running
in the lane you
have created just
for me

Dear Lord,

I pray that I would keep my eyes fixed on You and throw off all hindrances and distractions. I lay comparison at the foot of the Cross asking You to replace this entanglement with a heart of celebration and obedience. I pray that in those moments of looking side to side at what others are doing, You would remind me that there is room for all of us, no matter how similar the calling, because You have given each of us a unique voice through which to live out that calling.

Give me eyes to see myself the way You see me and the unique way You have gifted me. I pray that I would pursue ideas and dreams that are uniquely crafted by You for me and not be lured into imitating someone else's success. I pray that I would not allow comparison to paralyze me, and where it has I confess this to You and ask for healing and the encouragement I need to press on.

Help me to see the areas of my online life that cause me to struggle with comparison and show me where I need to set boundaries and disconnect. Search me and see if there is any jealousy and envy in me, and create in me a pure heart.

Instill in me an unwavering confidence in my calling, gifts, and purpose to withstand the distraction of comparison from the enemy. Where I have wished for someone else's story, gifts, or success, replace it with a desire for the celebration of being a part of Your bigger plan and humbled at being used in even the smallest way.

Lord, I want to bring glory to You in all that I do, and I know this cannot be done if I am consumed with looking at someone else's life and their highlight reels. Dear Jesus, keep my eyes fixed on You and keep me running in the lane You have created just for me.

———————

Because of this, the rumor spread among the believers that this disciple would not die. But Jesus did not say that he would not die; he only said, "If I want him to remain alive until I return, what is that to you?"
John 21:23 (NIV)

Am I now trying to win the approval of human beings, or of God? Or am I trying to please people? If I were still trying to please people, I would not be a servant of Christ.
Galatians 1:10 (NIV)

Do nothing from selfish ambition or conceit, but in humility count others more significant than yourselves.
Philippians 2:3 (ESV)

...let us throw off everything that hinders and the sin that so easily entangles. And let us run with perseverance the race marked out for us, fixing our eyes on Jesus, the pioneer and perfecter of faith.
Hebrews 12:1-2 (NIV)

Comparison is the paralyzer of dreams. Your calling, your purpose, and your dreams are yours. Hold on to them tight, because the enemy is going to try and steal them by convincing you they are not as worthy or as valuable as someone else's. And remember, that person you are comparing yourself to is probably struggling with comparison also. So let's start celebrating each other instead of comparing. The Lord can do so much more through us if we are not paralyzed.

———————

1. Pour out your heart to the Lord and confess to Him how you are struggling with comparison.

2. List the boundaries you need to set in your life, online or offline, to protect you against comparison.

3. Celebrate and praise the Lord for your unique calling, purpose, and gifts. Now celebrate and praise the Lord for that person you compare yourself to.

—— 21 ——
CONFIDENCE

Thank you for GODfidence & giving me permission to fully & unapologetically SHINE↓

Dear Lord,

You've placed in my heart these crazy dreams and desires. They seem so big and so far out of my reach. My deepest desire is to live a life soaked in significance—one that serves You and honors You. Despite my insecurities, I trust that You have given these dreams to me for such a time as this.

As I reflect upon the brave, brilliant, and bold women in the Bible, I ask that You help me to see myself as You saw them. Remove the pride and remove the pain as I relinquish the lies lingering from my past. I pray that You would show me my true beauty—the beauty found in my voice, grace, love, passion, persistence, and my willingness to surrender. Help me to remember that beauty is about alignment with divine assignment. Help me to boldly embrace and showcase my beauty like never before.

Let me bear much fruit—fruit that lasts and fruit that showcases what it means to grow from and in the tree of life.

Let me be a mighty vessel for miracles. Anchor me in wisdom, anointing, discernment, and love. Renew my mind such that I boldly believe I am all that you say I am as you stretch me and expand my territory. I know that my glory zone—the place where you are taking me—exists solely outside of my comfort zone.

Let me stand out, Lord. Let me unapologetically illuminate the brilliance, intellect, creativity, and diverse array of talent that You have intentionally deposited within me. All that I am, all I have, and all I am able to do comes from You. Remind me that my success is not about me but about You as the God who lives in me.

I am ready to manifest miracles, to be a producer, and to have an impact that leaves behind your magnificent imprint. Lord, when You said let there be light, thank you for giving me permission to shine.

And this is not your own doing; it is the gift of God, not a result of works, so that no one may boast. For we are his workmanship, created in Christ Jesus for good works, which God prepared in advance that we should do.

Ephesians 2:8-10 (ESV)

…let's just go ahead and be what we were made to be, without enviously or pridefully comparing ourselves with each other, or trying to be something we aren't.

Romans 12:6 (MSG)

The Angel Gabriel greeted Mary: Good morning! You're beautiful with God's beauty, Beautiful inside and out! God be with you. Mary was thoroughly shaken, wondering what was behind a greeting like that. But the angel assured her, "You have nothing to fear. God has a surprise for you!

Luke 1:28-30 (MSG)

Yes, I am the Vine; you are the branches. Whoever lives in me and I in him shall produce a large crop of fruit. For apart from me you can't do a thing. If anyone separates from me, he is thrown away like a useless branch, withers, and is gathered into a pile with all the others and burned. But if you stay in me and obey my commands, you may ask any request you like, and it will be granted! My true disciples produce bountiful harvests. This brings great glory to my Father.

John 15: 5-8 (TLB)

For some of us, a lack of confidence is the roadblock we face daily as we head out to run the race God has called us to. For others of us, we desperately search for the meaning of holy humility and what it looks like. The Lord has already told us who we are. Now we just need to believe Him.

———————————

1. Ask the Lord to reveal any lies or pain from your past that are chipping away at your confidence.

2. Ask the Lord to reveal what holy humility looks like as you pursue a life of confidence in Him and who He created you to be.

3. List out WHO God says you are and support it with scripture. Then prayerfully write out your own personal mission statement to include your story, your burden, your calling, and your gifts. This mission, combined with who God says you are, will be what you build your confidence on.

—— 22 ——
GOALS

Make the GOALS and DREAMS you
have for me plainly CLEAR.

Lord,

I surrender. I come to You right now with such a deep desire to accomplish the things that please You. Help me to give up my own goals and dreams in favor of Yours. Lord, please give me wisdom on what goals You would like me to pursue. Make the goals You have for me plainly clear. What do You want me to do with my time, resources, and the talents You've blessed me with? Whatever it is, help me to follow Your plans with abandon. Your plans are far better than my own. Help me to trust that and take action on Your leading and nothing else.

Please bind the enemy away from the path You've paved for me as I take action on these goals. Help me walk without fear of man but in reverent respect and fear of only You. Help me to meet my fears and surrender them completely as I trust in You and take action on what You have for me.

Lord, please help to surround me with fellow believers who will support me in taking action on the goals You have given me. Help me build close relationships with other sisters who want to live out Your plans too, Lord!

Give me the energy, wisdom, and endurance to take action on the goals You have for me. Help me to not be distracted by comparison, fear, or anything in this world. Keep my eyes fixed only on You, Father, as I make tiny steps forward and big leaps of faith.

Thank You, God, for giving us Your Word and wisdom so that we can be guided to know what our goals should be. You make it plain in Your word what You want us to focus on. Help me seek to build Your kingdom, not *my own. I love You so much! In Jesus's wonderful name, amen.*

———————

Trust in the Lord with all your heart and lean not on your own under-standing; in all your ways submit to him, and he will make your paths straight.
Proverbs 3:5-6 (NIV)

If any of you lacks wisdom, you should ask God, who gives generously to all without finding fault, and it will be given to you.
James 1:5 (NIV)

I press on toward the goal to win the prize for which God has called me heavenward in Christ Jesus.
Philippians 3:14 (NIV)

But seek first his kingdom and his righteousness, and all these things will be given to you as well.
Matthew 6:33 (NIV)

We approach each new year with big goals. When a dream is born, we charge ahead in pursuit of it. How awesome that we serve a God who wants to be involved in every plan and goal we set. What confidence and security we have in knowing He is the one who has already ordered our steps and our days. Let's sit at His feet and invite Him to be involved as we plan.

———————

1. Reflect on this last year and the goals you met. Celebrate and praise the Lord for His work in that accomplishment.

2. Go to the Lord and ask Him what goals He wants to set for you this month (and year).

3. List out action steps for this month that will help you achieve your God-given goals and pray over each one. Invite the Lord to be involved, provide discernment, and give direction.

—— 23 ——
CREATIVITY

Your beauty is everywhere, and I want to drink it up!

Heavenly Father,

Thank You for the way You've created me. You are the ultimate Creator, and I praise You for making me in your image. What an incredible gift to get to create! Lord, I just want to do right by You. I want to please You and glorify You with the things I make and the words I say. I want to help people feel special and loved and treasured through my work—to experience You more fully through my creations. I know that any skill I have comes directly from You, and I want to create work that brings You glory.

Sometimes I am scared that the ideas will stop coming. I pray that You would continue to bring me new inspiration and fresh ideas. I know that You have put beauty all around me, and I pray that You would open my eyes to see it. Surprise me today, Father. Reveal Yourself to me even in the smallest of moments. Lord, I pray that every relationship, conversation, thing I see, word I read, food I taste, and music I hear would be evidence of the beautiful world You've created for our enjoyment and inspiration.

Your beauty is everywhere, and I want to drink it up. You call us your masterpiece, Your workmanship. I know I am uniquely created, and I pray that I would create work from that place— work unique to me and unique to our partnership. Help me to not be tempted to create work that's unoriginal. You've given me a special gift, and I want to be true to and trust in that calling. Help me to not compare myself to others but to find comfort and joy in knowing that you have qualified me.

Every time I create something, I feel as though a piece of me has left. I feel exhilarated and exhausted and a little empty. Father, please fill back in those spaces. Fill me with Your love and mercy and gentleness and creativity. Fill me with Your strength and desire to do this all again tomorrow and the next day and the next. Sustain me, Lord, and give me a joyful heart! I praise You for the privilege of being a creator, and I thank You that we are in this business together. Every good and perfect gift comes from You, and I simply couldn't do it without You.

Amen.

So God created mankind in his own image, in the image of God he created them; male and female he created them.
Genesis 1:27 (NIV)

I have filled him with the Spirit of God, giving him great wisdom, ability, and expertise in all kinds of crafts.
Exodus 31:3 (NLT)

For we are God's handiwork, created in Christ Jesus to do good works, which God prepared in advance for us to do.
Ephesians 2:10 (NIV)

...and giving joyful thanks to the Father, who has qualified you to share in the inheritance of his holy people in the kingdom of light
Colossians 1:12 (NIV)

Every good and perfect gift is from above, coming down from the Father of the heavenly lights, who does not change like shifting shadow,
James 1:17 (NIV)

The beginning of every dream is full of creativity and inspiration. But there are moments in the midst of dreaming when we become weary, dry, and in need of fresh ideas. It can be tempting to look around at others for inspiration and find ourselves compromising through copying. Go to God, the creator and the giver of inspired and creative ideas, and see what He has reserved just for you.

―――――――――

1. Praise God for creating you in His image to be creative.

2. Confess any area of your work that has been a copy or too influenced by someone else's work. Pray that the Lord would keep your spirit sensitive to create with integrity.

3. Pray specifically for an area in your work or life that you desperately need the Lord to breathe creativity and newness into, creativity that is original to you.

—— 24 ——
STEWARDSHIP

it is not my own —
it is yours!
stuff will fade, but
you are forever.

God my Provider,

Thank You for the abundance You have placed in my hands. May I always view everything in my life as a gift from You that is simply to be managed for your kingdom. It is not my own—it is Yours! My prayer is that I would operate as a faithful steward, with open hands that are ready to receive and ready to give.

Lord, where my money is, my heart is there too. My bank accounts and budgets reflect my heart, and I want my heart to be pleasing to You! Break the chains of desire for stuff and give me a heart of contentment, Lord. Forgive me for ways I've neglected my financial responsibilities. Convict me to change my habits and do the hard work it requires to be a good steward. Holy Spirit, whisper this truth to me as I need to hear it: heaven and earth will pass away, but My words will not!

Stuff will fade, but You are forever.

Help me maintain a proper view of money. It is a tool that is used for Your kingdom and my provision. Give me the wisdom and self-discipline to always use my money for the good of Your kingdom. Oh that I would spend in wisdom and not on impulse, that I would save for opportunities that I cannot yet see, and that I would give generously in order to expand your purposes here on earth! By Your Spirit, give me the ability to manage well what I've been given, that I might show myself to be a good and faithful servant.

You alone, Lord, give me the ability to create wealth. Enlarge my territory, Lord, that I might be a mighty force for Your kingdom! As You have blessed me in every way, may I be generous in every way.

In the name of Jesus, give me a spirit of Stewardship. Amen.

———————

For where your treasure is, there your heart will be also.
Matthew 6:21 (ESV)

Know well the condition of your flocks, and give attention to your herds,
Proverbs 27:23 (ESV)

Jabez called upon the God of Israel, saying, "Oh that you would bless me and enlarge my border, and that your hand might be with me, and that you would keep me from harm so that it might not bring me pain!" And God granted what he asked.
1 Chronicles 4:10 (ESV)

Every good gift and every perfect gift is from above, coming down from the Father of lights with whom there is no variation or shadow due to change.
James 1:17 (ESV)

As followers of Christ, we know that our finances ultimately belong to God, so it's important that He finds us faithful not only in our spending but also in our giving. We should aspire to be good stewards of all He has given us.

———————

1. Do you have a monthly budget that you follow? If not, take some time to create one.

2. Are there areas in your financial stewardship that you struggle with? Confess them to God.

3. When it comes to finances, in what ways can you honor God? Ask Him to show you.

— 25 —
SUCCESS + FAILURE

Success is simply this.
l♥ve and obedience

Lord,

Thank You for being a God who gives us dreams. We hold them so close to our hearts, and we want them to succeed. Yet we also recognize that our ideas of "success" are so often different than Yours.

So we come to You and lay down our expectations, surrender our demands, and open our hearts and our hands. We will receive what You have for us. Give us Your perspective on what success truly means.

You are the God who spoke the world into being, and it's not hard for You to get things done. What You want most from us is not our efforts but our affection. Help us to remember that when we're tempted to strive for perfection. Remind us that success is simply this: love and obedience.

That means that when we say "yes" to You, we cannot fail, no matter how it may seem. No matter how we may feel. No matter what the world may say. Use that truth to free us from the fear of failure that so often holds us back. Help us to spread our wings, to take the risks, to never settle for anything less than Your very best.

At the end of our lives, we simply desire to hear this: "Well done, good and faithful servant." Nothing else matters. So may we live with love, joy, grace, and a determination to never give up on Your purpose for our lives.

Thank You for inviting us into the divine adventure of dreaming with You. We know what matters most is not the destination but what we'll share with You and others along the way. We look forward to what you will do in and through us.

To You be the glory of every success...

Amen.

———————

Trust in the Lord with all your heart; do not depend on your own understanding. Seek his will in all you do, and he will show you which path to take.
Proverbs 3:5-6 (NLT)

Take delight in the Lord, and he will give you your heart's desires.
Psalm 37:4 (NLT)

Many are the plans in a person's heart, but it is the Lord's purpose that prevails.
Proverbs 19:21 (NIV)

His master replied, "Well done, good and faithful servant! You have been faithful with a few things; I will put you in charge of many things. Come and share your master's happiness!"
Matthew 25:21 (NIV)

As we celebrate our successes and learn from our failures, it's important to know that God is at work and ever present in the midst of it all. We must seek His counsel and pursue His wisdom to know what path to take and to keep a godly perspective no matter the outcome, for He is sovereign in all things.

———————————

1. How do you define success in your own life? Ask God to align your definition of success with His purpose for you.

2. List all the ways God has shown Himself faithful in the midst of your failures.

3. What opportunities has God given you that have allowed you to succeed?

—— 26 ——
BUSYNESS

give me breath—
slow and spacious
and sweet

Dear God, forgive me for my busyness.

I know You take joy in my dreams. That You delight in seeing me explore my talents. I believe You are my champion in growing to soak up as much life as I can, in stretching to the very tips of my fingers and toes of who I was meant to be.

You love fullness - the fullness of being, feeling, exploring.

Yet when I'm drowning in busyness, I am not full. Instead of a bright, glorious day of sunshine and fresh air, full of possibility, I am a swirling tornado taking out others in my path with my lack of patience, compassion, care, time, and sensitivity. I am overly full, I have too much force, I am spinning faster than I can control.

I do not wear my busyness as a badge of honor.

I know that it is not a sign of my strength but my weakness, not my success but my striving, not my power but my lack of control, not my popularity but my disconnectedness.

I know this in my head, yet I fail to sketch it out in my daily life. God, give me eyes to see.

What matters most? What are the priorities? What do I need to let go of?

Why can I not breathe? I know that's not from You, so it must be something I can cast out and call for Your help to calm.

Am I choked by perfectionism? Smothered by pride? Weighted down by my inability to say no? Drowning in my vast appetite?

Grant me wisdom. Bless me with insight, aha moments, and the vision of how to make a shift. Put ideas, inspiration, and examples in my path. I've lived this way for so long that I don't know how to begin to change. Guide my path, my heart, and my desires. Make me less of who I desire to be and more of who You desire me to be. Help me to be someone who sprints less and savors more. Give me breath that is slow and spacious and sweet. In your Son's name, amen.

The Lord will fight for you; you need only to be still.
Exodus 14:14 (NIV)

God met me more than halfway, he freed me from my anxious fears ...
Worship God if you want the best; worship opens all doors to His
goodness ...Who out there has a lust for life? ...Embrace peace -- don't let
it get away! ...Is anyone crying for help? God is listening, ready to rescue
you. If your heart is broken, you'll find God right there;if you're kicked
in the gut, he'll help you catch your breath."
Psalms 34 (excerpts from MSG)

I will do what you have asked. I will give you a wise and discerning heart.
1 Kings 3:12 (NIV)

Comfort, comfort my people, says your God ...
He will not grow tired or weary, and his understanding no one can fath-
om. He gives strength to the weary and increases the power of the weak.
Isaiah 40: 1, 28-29 (NIV)

It's easy to glorify our busy schedules. We think that if our day is packed and people need us, then we are successful. But in our busyness, we can neglect the people and passions that really matter.

————————————

1. What does your day typically look like? Write out your daily schedule.

2. List all the "time wasters" in your day that you need to either let go of completely or set time restraints on. (e.g., social media, cell phone, tardiness)

3. It's important to create boundaries to balance your work and home life. What boundaries and changes can you implement in your day that will allow you more time to pour into family and friends?

27

MY BUSINESS

MAY
WHATEVER
YOU DO IN
WORD OR
DEED
BE DONE
IN THE
NAME OF YOUR
PRECIOUS
SON

Dearest Heavenly Father,

I praise You for always doing immeasurably more than I could ever dream possible. Thank You for entrusting me with the gift of this business. Every good and perfect gift is from above, coming down from You. Please make me a good steward of this amazing gift. I know that to whom much is given, much is required. Equip me to be a good leader and to run this business well. Teach me to dream bigger, to follow the direction of the Holy Spirit, and to execute His leading with excellence.

Thank You for each client and customer You bring. I pray that everything we create and every vision that is cast may bless, encourage, and point people toward You. Let every detail attest to Your goodness, Your majesty, Your creativity, Your faithfulness, Your power, and Your love. Help me show Your love and mercy to our customers, our clients, our suppliers, and everyone else You send our way.

Teach me to know when to give grace and when to stand firm in principle. Fill me with the confidence to hold fast to my convictions, the humility to admit my mistakes, and the wisdom to learn from them. I pray that others would see something different in our work; that they would see YOU. I pray that my business would not become an idol or where I place my worth but that it would stay in its rightful place—submitted to You.

Please give me the strength to share my faith boldly. Use my story to reach the lost and to plant a seed of hope. May whatever we do in word or deed be done in the name of Your precious Son. I pray that all will feel welcomed but will leave changed.

In the powerful name of Jesus, amen.

———————————

Now to him who is able to do immeasurably more than all we ask or imagine, according to his power that is at work within us,
Ephesians 3:20 (NIV)

Every good and perfect gift is from above, coming down from the Father of the heavenly lights, who does not change like shifting shadows.
James 1:17 (NIV)

Jesus replied: " 'Love the Lord your God with all your heart and with all your soul and with all your mind.' This is the first and greatest commandment. And the second is like it: 'Love your neighbor as yourself.' "
Matthew 22: 37-39 (NIV)

And we all, who with unveiled faces contemplate the Lord's glory, are being transformed into his image with ever-increasing glory, which comes from the Lord, who is the Spirit.
2 Corinthians 3:18 (NIV)

Running a business can sometimes feel like birthing and rais-
ing a child. Days and nights are full of hard work, big dreams,
loss of sleep, fear of the unknown, and joyful celebration. God
cares about every single detail. Our business is often the place
where our gifts, purpose, and calling intersect, so let's pursue
excellence and choose grace as we build them.

————————

1. What is a strength or gift the Lord has given you that makes your
business stand apart from others? Give thanks to the Lord.

2. Ask the Lord to show you what is next for your business—that
big idea, new product, collaboration, or opportunity.

3. Pray for 3 of your competitors. Ask the Lord to bless their business. (Yes, we said "bless")

28

BRANDING + MARKETING

May my brand be a foundation to a thriving business that glorifies you Lord Jesus.

Dear Lord,

You know who I am. You created me and have given me these gifts.

I pray that my brand would signify trustworthiness and purpose. I pray that people would see my story as one of hope and perseverance, and please, Lord, protect it from any negativity. Help me, God, to deliver my message clearly, that those who intersect with my dream feel encouraged. Lord, allow people to understand why I do this. Holy Spirit, show me how to stand out from the others, to have my own unique story that fills those who hear it with hope and inspiration.

Father, let my work speak truth and loyalty while residing within the hearts of those it reaches. May my brand be a foundation to a thriving business that glorifies You, Lord Jesus. Lord, I pray You would help me to stand against all that the enemy wants to throw at me.

Lead me, Holy Spirit, into all that You have for my business. Connect people to my work emotionally; allow them to feel Your love through it.

God, I pray that my brand would be strong and stand up against those who mean harm. Help me to hear Your voice in those moments of uncertainty.

Lord, give my brand significance in the marketplace, all the while keeping me humble.

Thank You, wonderful God, for the gifts You gave me. Help me to use my gifts for good things, while attracting and retaining a loyal following. Enable me to grow and make wise decisions, even when I fail.

Empower me to use my brand to help others so that they may find their purpose in You. I continue to wait for Your direction, oh Lord. In Jesus's name I pray. Amen.

————————

Whether you turn to the right or to the left, your ears will hear a voice behind you, saying, "This is the way; walk in it."
Isaiah 30:21 (NIV)

for God's gifts and his call are irrevocable.
Romans 11:29 (NIV)

Not only so, but we also glory in our sufferings, because we know that suffering produces perseverance;
Romans 5:3 (NIV)

God is within her, she will not fall; God will help her at break of day
Psalm 46:5 (NIV)

Whether you are in the process of creating your brand or in the middle of living it out, the process can be an opportunity for the enemy to come in and create confusion, comparison, and distraction. First, understanding and finding confidence in your "why" is the foundation for any solid brand and will keep you focused as the tides of business, competition, and opportunities change. God even cares about the seemingly little details of logos, colors, and websites, so choose to prayerfully walk through this process as you seek vendors to align with who will help you execute the core of your brand.

————————

1. Pray and journal about your "why" and ask the Lord for clarity and confidence.

2. Confess any confusion, comparison, or distraction about your brand and ask the Lord to reveal to you the unique story behind your dream.

3. List out and pray over the things you need to accomplish to physically launch your brand message.

29

COLLABORATION + OPPORTUNITY

Help me not to be so
focused on my plans that
I miss opportunities
you've laid before me.

Dear Father,

I'm so grateful for the opportunities that I have to serve You while using the gifts You've given me—especially when it involves working alongside others. It's so encouraging to see a group of people with different, unique abilities coming together and collaborating on a project. It's in moments of opportunities and collaboration that I can't help but praise you for granting me the desires of my heart and partnering me with like-minded believers!

Still, there are times when my focus shifts from You to the plans I have for myself. Forgive me for the times that I idolize these opportunities. May I be able to keep these collaborations and opportunities in an eternal perspective and understand that in everything I do, seemingly big or small, my ultimate purpose on earth is to bring You glory and share Your Gospel message.

Lord, please open up doors of opportunity for me. I earnestly seek to use my gifts for Your glory. But I also pray for contentment if You choose not to give me what I ask of You right now. Help me to trust that You are sovereign and have a perfect plan for my life. Help me to not be so focused on my plans that I miss the opportunities You've laid before me.

God, when opportunity does come my way, please keep me humble. Remind me that every opportunity is because of You. Protect me from a mind-set that believes anything else.

When collaborating with others, please give me a servant's heart. Help me to recognize the needs of those around me and to know how to serve them well. May I learn to give my gifts freely and offer them to others without hesitation.

Allow me to be discerning with my time. Give me wisdom with when to say yes and when to say no to collaboration and opportunities. May these opportunities never get in the way of my time with You or my other first callings.

Thank You for the Church body and for the importance that comes with each and every role. What a beautiful sight to see us all exercising our gifts in the different ways You've called us to. May it all be for Your glory.

In Jesus's name, amen.

The heart of man plans his way, but the Lord establishes his steps.
Proverbs 16:9 (ESV)

So, whether you eat or drink, or whatever you do, do all to the glory of God.
1 Corinthians 10:31 (ESV)

For as in one body we have many members, and the members do not all have the same function, so we, though many, are one body in Christ, and individually members one of another.
Romans 12:4-5 (ESV)

From whom the whole body, joined and held together by every joint with which it is equipped, when each part is working properly, makes the body grow so that it builds itself up in love.
Ephesians 4:16 (ESV)

The Lord gives us the opportunity to collaborate with others as a way to serve His people, so it's important that we pray and ask God to lead us in all opportunities and do all works with a servant's heart.

———————————

1. List the people that God has put on your heart to collaborate with. If no one comes to mind, pray and ask God to reveal them to you.

2. Take some time to pray for protection and discernment as opportunities come your way, that you would be careful not to pursue out of selfish desires or say "yes" without prayerful consideration.

3. What collaborations has the Lord allowed you to be a part of in the past that have blessed others? Write them out and take some time to reflect on His faithfulness.

—— 30 ——
ONLINE INFLUENCE

Mostly Lord,
I just open my hands
to you and say — its yours.
My words, my
thoughts, any sphere of
influence I have
online — do with
it what you
will.

Lord,

You're the real King of the internet. It's Yours, and it's an amazing playground for Your people to proclaim Your Kingdom. You are good and have been good long before someone ever called You good on Instagram. Help us to see how wonderful and beautiful and Holy You are. Help us to be more overwhelmed with You than we are with any other thing.

Lord, I confess I've made the internet and online influence about me time and time and time again. Instead of pointing to You—or sometimes even while I'm pointing to You—I've made it about me and who likes me or what they feel about me. Forgive me. Help set my heart on a path that longs and thirsts for You way more than it thirsts for the approval of others.

Father, I ask that by the work of the Holy Spirit in me and online, you would make Your name great. I pray that You'd increase the number of those who call on You and that You'd increase my ability to articulate the truths You've put in my heart and the story You've given me to share for Your Name's sake.

Mostly, Lord, I just open my hands to You and say it's Yours. My words, my thoughts, any sphere of influence I have online—do with it what You will. Speak clearly and help me to listen intently to what it is You want me to do and follow that. I want to be a woman who knows Jesus above all else, much more than I want to be known myself.

...and to make it your ambition to lead a quiet life: You should mind your own business and work with your hands, just as we told you,
1 Thess 4:11 (NIV)

But you are a chosen people, a royal priesthood, a holy nation, God's special possession, that you may declare the praises of him who called you out of darkness into his wonderful light.
1 Peter 2:9 (NIV)

LORD, I have heard of your fame; I stand in awe of your deeds, LORD. Repeat them in our day, in our time make them known; in wrath remember mercy.
Habakkuk 3:2 (NIV)

He must become greater; I must become less.
John 3:30 (NIV)

Influence is not a bad thing… Jesus had a lot of it. But if not handled prayerfully, we can make it all about ourselves and obsess over building our popularity, ultimately allowing our "fame" to become an idol. Let's give Him our platforms and our influence and wait upon Him to give back and expand what ultimately brings Him the most glory. We don't want it any other way, and we definitely do not want to build an influence that replaces God's influence in our lives.

———————

1. Celebrate and praise the Lord for the influence and platform He has given you, no matter how big or small, and how He has used it thus far to point people to the gospel through your words and actions.

2. Have you focused more on building your influence than building God's kingdom?

3. Have you found your value and worth in your level of influence or lack of influence?

—— 31 ——
SOCIAL MEDIA

Jesus, help me remember
that it's in you alone
that I find my significance —
not in my fans, followers
or my platform.

Dear Lord,

Fill me with Your Spirit in a new way today. Give me the wisdom to look at all of my social media through the lens of your eternal perspective. Give me the strength and discipline to be a good steward of my time and talents and to always remember that my life and my words are a reflection of You.

Jesus, help me remember that it's in You alone that I find my significance—not in my fans, followers, or my platform.

Search me, O God, and know my heart; test me and know my anxious thoughts. See if there is any offensive way in me, and lead me in the way everlasting. (Psalm 139:23 NIV)

Holy Spirit, examine my heart and realign any motives that are not pure or of You. I praise You that You cleanse me from all impurities and from all of my idols. Give me the clarity to hold up each social network and examine if it is an idol. Give me the boldness to ask: Is this life-giving to me? Does this bring God glory? Do I use it to share His love with others?

Help me remember that the world and things in it are sifting sand. Help me to not get caught up in the comparison game or be ashamed that I'm a follower of Jesus, but give me the boldness to proclaim the Gospel. (Romans 1:16)

Teach me to do Your will, for You are my God; may Your good Spirit lead me on level ground. (Psalm 143:10 NIV)

I pray that through all things in my life You would do immeasurably more than I could ask or imagine. May my life be worthy of You, Lord, and please You in every way, bearing good fruit that honors You. Empower me with Your Spirit to share the unique testimony that You have given me, both in my community and online.

Thank You for giving me Your Son, Jesus, and it's in His precious name I pray, amen.

For this reason, since the day we heard about you, we have not stopped praying for you. We continually ask God to fill you with the knowledge of his will through all the wisdom and understanding that the Spirit gives, so that you may live a life worthy of the Lord and please him in every way: bearing fruit in every good work, growing in the knowledge of God, being strengthened with all power according to his glorious might so that you may have great endurance and patience, and giving joyful thanks to the Father, who has qualified you to share in the inheritance of his holy people in the kingdom of light. For he has rescued us from the dominion of darkness and brought us into the kingdom of the Son he loves, in whom we have redemption, the forgiveness of sins.

Colossians 1:9-14 (NIV)

...let your light shine before others, so thatb they may see your good works and give glory to your Father who is in heaven.

Matthew 5:14-16 (ESV)

I pray that out of his glorious riches he may strengthen you with power through his Spirit in your inner being, so that Christ may dwell in your hearts through faith. And I pray that you, being rooted and established in love, may have power, together with all the Lord's holy people, to grasp how wide and long and high and deep is the love of Christ, and to know this love that surpasses knowledge—that you may be filled to the measure of all the fullness of God. Now to him who is able to do immeasurably more than all we ask or imagine, according to his power that is at work within us,

Ephesians 3:16-20 (NIV)

In the world today, social media is often at the forefront of our lives. We check it first thing in the morning and right before bed. If we're not careful, it can consume us. We have to be intentional to use this platform for good. We must ask God to give us strength and discipline to be good stewards of our time and the words we post. We want our online lives to be a reflection of His work in our lives.

———————————

1. Are you using social media to influence in a positive way? List all the ways that you can be a light to the online world.

2. Do you fall into comparison when looking at the online profiles of others? If so, confess your struggles to God and ask for freedom in this area.

3. Do you find yourself obsessing over the number of followers or likes you have? What actions can you take to create boundaries so that social media does not become an idol in your life?

shine like stars

On behalf of all of the women who offered prayers and insight in these pages, thank you. Thank you for desiring a closer relationship with God. That encourages us all! Keep seeking Him through His word and through prayer and community with other believers—what a gift. If you don't have a community to support you yet, we pray that God will open doors for you to find close friends who love Him and can walk this journey with you. We pray that we would all shine like stars, reflecting His glory, as we hold out the word of life, as it says in Philippians 2:15. We pray that we all not just talk to God in prayer and listen to His word but ACT on it.

Lord, we praise You for Your very Good News and that You hear our prayers! May our lives—our words, our actions, and all of our prayers—honor You. Give us wisdom to use the prayers in this book as a way to connect more deeply with You in order to live each of our days here on this earth on purpose. Help us to dream big for You! We love You!

THE CONTRIBUTORS
the dreamers + the doers

JENN SPRINKLE
Burden of a Dream,
Comparison Prayer,
Chapter Devotionals &
Questions

Jenn is an outgoing introvert married to her equally dream-driven husband, Jon. She is a recovering serial entrepreneur, speaker, champion of the risk taker and owner of a small graphic design and web studio. She and her husband share a heart for hurting marriages and living simple and missionally. As cofounder of The {well} Studio, her burden is for discouraged dreamers and weary entrepreneurs, with a desire to encourage and equip them to pursue without distraction their calling and purpose that brings glory to God.

Dallas, Texas // jennsprinkle.com + thewellstudio.co

KELLY RUCKER
A Call to Surrender,
Seasons Prayer,
Chapter Devotionals &
Questions

As cofounder of The {well} Studio, Kelly Rucker's mission is to uplift women in all seasons of life, ultimately leading them back to the Cross. Kelly is a photographer who resides in beautiful Austin, Texas, with her husband, Kevin; daughter, Robin Holiday; and poodle pup, Mardy. Kelly believes love and servanthood are the greatest callings in her life. When she is not visually storytelling through photography, she can be found spending time with family and friends, traveling, eating sushi, and drinking red wine—preferably all at the same time!

Austin, Texas // kellyrucker.com + thewellstudio.co

JENNIE ALLEN
Foreward

Jennie Allen is the award- winning and bestselling author of the books *Anything* and *Restless,* as well as the Bible studies *Stuck, Chase, and Restless.* The founder and visionary for the IF: Gathering, she is a passionate leader following God's call on her life to catalyze a generation of women to live what they believe. Jennie has a Master's in Biblical Studies from Dallas Theological Seminary and lives in Austin, Texas, with her husband, Zac, and four children, Connor, Kate, Caroline and Cooper.

Austin, Texas // jennieallen.com + ifgathering.

DEMI
AUSTIN-THOMAS
My Spouse's Dreams +
My Children's Dreams

Demi Austin-Thomas is a national TV personality, certified parent coach, and empowerment thought speaker. Her heart and vision is to extract the greatness out of the lives of others, empowering them to pursue their passion and purpose. She is passionate about family and parenting and finds joy in coaching parents on how to bridge the gap in their relationships with their teens. She is wife to James and mother to three beautiful and imperfect children.

Dallas, Texas // demitheparentcoach.com

CHELSIE BIRKS
Identity

Chelsie Birks is a highly accomplished national makeup artist turned stylist who brings a rare and unique Christian perspective to the A-list world of fashion and beauty. As a speaker and a writer, her heart is to empower women to authentically live the journey of their beautifully messy lives. Her greatest passion is helping others discover not only who they are, but also who's they are.

Dallas, Texas // myglossylife.com + chelsiebirks.com

MEGAN BURNS
Serving

Megan Burns is a lover of Jesus, a wife, a mother of five, and a creative entrepreneur. She is the founder of She Does Justice, an online boutique that gives a portion of sales to a different cause each month. One of her biggest passions is helping women to believe that they can make a difference.

Phoenix, Arizona // shedoesjustice.com

LARA CASEY
Goals + Afterword

Lara Casey is a believer in the "impossible." She is the publisher and editor-in-chief of Southern Weddings, which encourages couples to plan a meaningful beginning to married life. Lara's first book, Make it Happen: Surrender Your Fear, Take the Leap, Live on Purpose, released in December 2014 (Thomas Nelson Publishers). She frequently speaks on goal-setting, mission-centered business, and faith. Lara lives in Chapel Hill, NC, with her husband and daughter, Grace.

Chapel Hill, North Carolina // laracasey.com

LAUREN CHANDLER
Worship + Gratitude

Lauren Chandler is a wife and mother of three. She leads worship regularly at The Village Church in Flower Mound, Texas, where her husband, Matt, is the lead teaching pastor. Whether writing songs or stories, singing, or making her home a place to linger, Lauren enjoys creating beautiful and meaningful spaces where people may encounter the Lord of steadfast love imaged perfectly through Jesus.

Dallas, Texas // laurenchandler.com

Jess Connolly is a gal in the grip of God's grace. She's an entrepreneur, author, and speaker who lives in Charleston, South Carolina, with her four wild kids and her church-planting husband. She is passionate about this generation of women intimately knowing God, His Word, and their beautiful inheritance found in His Kingdom.

JESS CONNOLLY
Online Influence

Charleston, South Carolina // jessconnolly.com + naptimediariesshop.com

Reinvention Strategist, Influence Expert & Godfidence® Coach Marshawn Evans Daniels has a passion for mentoring women influencers of faith to find their voice, believe bigger, and live bigger. As a former Miss America finalist and Donald Trump Apprentice turned million-dollar Womanprenuer Faith + Business Coach, she teaches on manifestation, gift maximization, peak performance, brand monetization, and marketplace mastery to coaches, speakers, authors, celebrities, professional athletes, and everyday women ready to walk in full alignment with their divine assignment.

MARSHAWN DANIELS
Confidence

Atlanta, Georgia // marshawn.com + godfidence.com

Holley Gerth is a best-selling author, certified life coach, and speaker who enjoys encouraging the hearts of women through words. She'd love to have coffee with you and cheer you on in your dreams. Until then, she hopes you'll hang out with her at holleygerth.com.

Fayetteville, Arkansas // holleygerth.com

HOLLEY GERTH
Success + Failure

TRICIA GOYER
Dreams

USA Today best-selling author Tricia Goyer is the author of 45 books and over 500 articles for national publications. She blogs for high-traffic sites like TheBetterMom.com and MomLifeToday.com. Tricia loves to inspire women to tell their unique stories and follow big God-dreams. Tricia and her husband, John, live in Little Rock, Arkansas. They have six fantastic children, a lovely daughter-in-law, and two adorable grandchildren.

Little Rock, Arkansas // triciagoyer.com

ESTHER HAVENS
Fears

Esther Havens is a humanitarian photographer capturing stories around the world that transcend a person's circumstances and reveal their true strength. Her images compel thought and challenge action. At heart, she is a connector, fostering relationships across continents, cultures, industries and perspectives. When not traveling, Esther is currently home-based in Dallas, TX at WELD.

Dallas, Texas // estherhavens.com

CLAIRE HOGAN
Loving {Well}

Claire McCormack Hogan is a national food photographer based in Dallas, Texas. Her clients range from worldwide brands to neighborhood restaurants, and her desire is to tell the story behind the food, the art, and the people she photographs. When she's not behind the camera, Claire's heart is to pour into the people around her, most importantly her husband Ben and new daughter, Charlotte.

Dallas, Texas // clairemccormack.com

DIANNE JAGO
God's Word and Collaboration + Opportunity

Dianne Jago is the founder of Deeply Rooted Magazine, a military wife, and mama of two who is just trying to live her day-to-day all for the glory of God. Since surrendering her life to the Lord, she has had an unrelenting passion to encourage other Christians to live life with eternity in view and to help them build a firm foundation by pointing them back to the Bible. Dianne's heart for the dreamer and doer is that he or she would seek God with heart, mind, and soul.

Lancaster, Pennsylvania // diannejago.com + deeplyrootedmag.com

ALISA KEETON
Wellness

Alisa Keeton is a woman of crazy-big faith and is passionately committed to serving the Lord. After twenty plus years as a fitness professional, Alisa felt the call from God to bring new meaning into the world of fitness and wellness. At first she resisted, but eventually God got his way. She got on her knees, rolled up her sleeves, followed the call, and in 2007 Revelation Wellness® was born.

Phoenix, Arizona // revelationwellness.org

REBEKAH LYONS
Faith

Rebekah Lyons is a mother of three, wife of one, and dog walker of two living in Nashville. She's an old soul with a contemporary, honest voice who puts a new face on the struggles women face as they seek to live a life of meaning. As a self-confessed mess, Rebekah wears her heart on her sleeve, which is a benefit to friends and readers alike.

Nashville, Tennessee // rebekahlyons.com

KRISTEN STEELE McCALL
Social Media

Kristen McCall believes in wild authenticity and has been gripped by the life-changing power of Jesus. She's a writer, marketing professional, social media strategist, entrepreneur, and speaker who lives in Nashville, Tennessee, with her toddler and husband, Justin. Her mission is to help others have the courage to be authentically who they are and use the gifts that God has given them to love others well.

Nashville, Tennessee // graciouslyauthentic.com

JILL MONACO
Freedom

Jill is the founder of a non profit and is passionate about encouraging people to pursue the presence of God. She frequently speaks on singleness, taking radical leaps of faith and freedom in Christ. She's the publisher and editor-in-chief of the online magazine for Christian singles over 30, Single Matters®. As a Freedom Life Coach she meets weekly with clients helping them experience the love of God in the midst of the circumstances of life.

Dallas, Texas // jillmonaco.com + singlematters.com

AEDRIEL MOXLEY
Rest + Balance

Aedriel Moxley is passionate about helping women see that they are living the life God designed specifically for their hearts and unique capabilities. As an artist, ceramist, designer, wife and mom, Aedriel understands the challenge of balancing it all. Founder of Aedriel.com 'Finding Grace In the Everyday', she encourages women to find beauty, even in the midst of the mess, while resting in the assurance that we're all right where we're supposed to be.

Albuquerque, New Mexico // aedriel.com

BETH ANN PLATT
Singleness

Beth Ann Platt is an artist, dreamer, coffee lover, DIY-er, and writer. While she used to be a California girl, she now considers Maryland home. In 2013, Beth Ann established an art shop, Elleizahbeth, where she loves nothing more than making Jesus known through her art. When she isn't working on her latest art pieces, she is serving on the team at Thryve Magazine. Beth Ann's desire is to celebrate Jesus in every moment, seek Him most in her singleness, and radiate His light and love in all that she does.

Gaithersburg, Maryland // elleizahbeth.com + thryvemag.com

NANCY RAY
Stewardship

Nancy Ray is a wife, blogger, photographer, and speaker. She lives her life and runs her photography business with the belief that it's all her ministry. Nancy speaks regularly about her faith, business, and financial stewardship in order to help others discover their purpose: to live out their calling and to manage their finances in a way that increases God's kingdom on the earth. She lives in Raleigh with her husband, Will, and great dane, Winston.

Raleigh, North Carolina // nancyrayphotography.com

JEN RAMOS
Branding + Marketing

Jen Ramos is a New York City-based graphic designer who owns the online shop MadeByGirl and authors the Made By Girl blog. Her passion for art led her to launch her own online gallery, Cocoa & Hearts, where she sells her original paintings. Jen's work has been featured in many popular home decor magazines, yet she remains humble and passionate about helping those in need. She loves looking for ways to glorify God through her work.

New York, New York // madebygirl.com

KRISTIN ROGERS
Grace in my Home

Kristin Rogers is a natural light photographer and artist based in Southern California. Her heart does a "pitter-patter" for nature, adoption, reading, coffee, homeschooling, thrift shops, messy hair, and road trips. She's still giddy over her husband of twelve years and adores her two daughters who make her life both joyful and messy. She desires for herself and others to find the beauty in the everyday—the dishes, the ripped dress, the trials of life—and seeks to wrap it all up in God's grace and still be able to smile.

Fullerton, California // kristinrogersphotography.

HILARY RUSHFORD
Busyness

Founder of Dean Street Society, Hilary Rushford is a personal stylist and mentor of fellow entrepreneurs. She's passionate about crafting lives with more joy and authentic confidence through education plus empathy. Hilary believes in creating providence — pursuing excellence so God can fling open the doors meant for you — living in the sweet spot of gumption and grace. She's passionate about bow ties, brunches and bold lipstick.

Brooklyn, New York // deanstreetsociety.com

LINDSAY
SHERBONDY
Creativity

Lindsay Sherbondy is a graphic designer turned calligrapher and an avid dreamer turned creative entrepreneur. She loves Jesus, spending time with her husband and little girl, iced coffee, authenticity, making beautiful things, and worshiping through creating.

Nashville, Tennessee // lindsayletters.com

MEGAN SMALLEY
Business

Megan Smalley is a Texan by birth and an Alabamian by marriage. She met and fell in love with her husband of three years while cheering at Auburn University. She is a coach's wife, entrepreneur, business owner of Scarlet & Gold and a photographer. Megan has a huge heart for encouraging people through business to love each other, chase after Jesus and be excellent at what they do.

Auburn, Alabama // scarletandgoldshop.com

MAGGIE WHITLEY
Simplicity

Maggie Whitley is a wife, mama, blogger, and handmade business owner living in Los Angeles. She and her family live in a cozy apartment and are on a mission to live a less busy life. After traveling to Tanzania, Africa (May 2012), Maggie and her husband, Zack, felt the LORD calling them to be more adventurous but with less possessions, which leads to their passion for simple living.

Los Angeles, California // maggiewhitley.com

CASEY WIEGAND
Motherhood

Casey Wiegand is married to her best friend, Christopher, and is mom to a five-year-old boy, Aiden; a four-year-old girl, Ainsleigh; and a two-year-old, Apple. Writing and sharing Christ is a true passion of hers, and being able to share her life and thoughts through her online space has been an amazing journey so far. She is a free spirit and has a heart for Jesus and for women pursuing their purpose and passions. She desperately wants to encourage others and love people well.

Dallas, Texas // thewiegands.com

FRANCIE WINSLOW
Marriage

Francie is the author of The God Experience: A Ten Week Guide to Feed Your Busy Soul. With a Masters Degree in Evangelism and Leadership from Wheaton College, she speaks and writes on topics that help others live connected to the heart of God in the midst of their real lives. Her real life is currently full to the brim as she mothers four little ones and dares to believe that families (specifically marriages) were designed by God to be a reflection of heaven on earth. Francie and her husband are consistently amazed by the faithfulness of God as they pray for His kingdom to come in their everyday lives just as it is in heaven.

Washington, DC // franciewinslow.com

VALERIE WOERNER
Prayer

Valerie Woerner is the owner of Val Marie Paper and the creator of the VMP Prayer Journal. She lives in Southern Louisiana, with her husband, Tyler, and little girl, Vivi Mae. She loves inspiring women to live lives of peace and joy through her paper products and blog.

Lafayette, Louisiana // valmariepaper.com

GINA ZEIDLER
Authenticity

Gina Zeidler is a photographer, momma, wife, mentor, encourager, and connector. But most importantly, she is a child of God. She loves serving others through the gifts and avenues she has been given. Encouraging others through sharing real life is where she finds true joy, because through our messy, Jesus shines through.

Twin Cities, Minnesota // ginazeidler.com

The {well} Studio was launched in 2014 to gather a community of women to encourage, inspire and equip them on their journey of entrepreneurship, dreaming and doing in response to how God has uniquely called each of us. We desire to extend grace to ourselves and others and instead of trying to do it all – we simply desire to work, live and love well...*not perfectly, but {well}*.

'Well done, my good and faithful servant. You have been faithful in handling this small amount, so now I will give you many more responsibilities. Let's celebrate together!'
Matthew 25:21 (NLT)

thewellstudio.co

CHRISTINE
GARRISON
*The {well} Studio Team
-Special Projects-*

Christine Garrison is a military spouse who loves the Lord and the blessing of being a wife. She spends her time in the kitchen baking, fly-fishing on the river, stopping in every antique store she lays eyes on, and using snail mail to keep in touch with friends. She adores working with The {well} Studio because it has connected her to some amazing women and allowed her to be a part of a group that encourages steady progress through the joys and difficulties of entrepreneurship. Through God's grace and for His glory, she tries to live each day by four simple words: love God, love people.

DuPont, Washington

CYNTHIA MASELLI
*The {well} Studio Team
-Special Projects-*

Cynthia Maselli is a wife, mom, writer, and founder of Just Relax. Candle + Co. Cynthia enjoys life in Southern California with her husband and their son. She loves being a part of The {well} Studio among a community of faith-filled entrepreneurs where she gets to do what she loves: share stories about inspirational women and connect with others to encourage, inspire, and support them on their journeys in life.

San Diego, California // justrelaxcandleco.com

204

ACKNOWLEDGEMENTS

Lord, what an adventure You have had us on. Thank You for loving us, showing us mercy and grace and gifting us with creativity and ideas that inspire us to point people to You. Thank You for burdening our hearts for this community of women who dream and do and love You deeply.

Thank You, Lord, for gifting us the idea for this book of prayers. For designing an amazing path of connections and relationships over the past several years with the women who came together with us to write this book. Thank You for moving in their hearts to say "yes" and write inspiring prayers for your dreamers and doers.

To the contributors, the women who came alongside us and caught the vision of this project with excitement, we thank you. Thank you for entrusting us with your God-inspired prayers. Thank you for sharing this project with your own community of dreamers and doers. Our prayer is that you might experience the Lord in a new and deeply intimate way this year and increasingly more in the years to come. We hope we can give each of you a HUGE hug some day....if we haven't already!

──────── ACKNOWLEDGEMENTS ────────

To our publisher, Kennisha of Nyree Press. I am so thankful that you came into our lives at just the right time. Thank you for not being afraid of our timeline and believing that God could do this! And to Amanda, our editor, thank you for your patience. There were so many moving parts. Thank you Michelle McKinney for combing through these pages when you didn't have to and sharing additional edits.

To the Givingtons Team. Thank you, Allen Befort, for believing in this project and creating the perfect logistical plan that supports both our contributors and their nonprofits.

The {well} Studio community. You have grown with us, encouraged us, and supported us as we have hopefully encouraged and supported you. Thank you for your patience as we have navigated building a community and all that it requires. Our ideas and dreams for you are so big and a huge reason this devotional was birthed. And thank you for the team of volunteers all over the country who have given their time, hearts, and energy to help build this community.

To Christine and Cynthia, you have lead within our team, taken ownership in our vision and become dear friends. Thank you for believing in these women and sharing our burden for them.

xoxo - Jenn Sprinkle and Kelly Rucker

──────── FROM JENN SPRINKLE ────────

Lord, I give you praise. Without You all my dreaming is in vain. What patience and mercy you show me daily. Thank you for the beautiful mess of a story you have given me that has your grace and redemption written all over it.

My husband, Jon. You have waded through the waters of my multiple dreams and businesses. You have shown patience beyond measure. You are my cheerleader, my ultimate dream defender, and my gypsy soul mate. IHY.

To my father-in-law. My heart is so sad that you are not here. So many times I wanted to call you up, seek your wisdom, and make sure my theology was correct. I believed I could do this book because of you. I miss you.

To my mom. You have always been my biggest fan through every crazy idea, dream, success, and failure. Always. My sister, who is my constant. Thank you for blessing me with Bennett and Ryder, the next best thing to having my own children. And to the best aunt, uncle and cousins a girl could ask for, thank you for loving me in spite of my crazy dreams and crazier life.

To Kelly Rucker. I needed a dream defender and a partner in crime, and you accepted the challenge. Thank you for your patience with my millions of ideas, helping me keep my eyes fixed on Jesus and reminding me of our "why". *(and of course all of the hilarious notes)*

To my other dream defenders: the others who have cheered me on, believed in me, encouraged me, pushed me, and have told me *"it's worth it, you were made for this"*: Jeni, Claire, Jennie, Robin, Ashley and Shelly & Tim. I love you all.

───── FROM KELLY RUCKER ─────

I give praise and thanksgiving to my heavenly Father. Thank You, Lord, for loving me unconditionally, for saving me, and for showing me grace on a daily basis. You have refined my heart and given me purpose. You are my everything.

To my husband and best friend, Kevin. You have shown me the true meaning of love. Thank you for supporting me and encouraging me in all that I do. I am the luckiest girl in the world to be by your side.

To my daughter, Robin Holiday. It's an honor and privilege to be your mom. You are the greatest little gift God ever gave me! Thank you for being mine.

To my partner in crime, Jenn. My life is richer because of you. Thank you for pushing me to be my best, challenging me to think outside the box, and for reminding me that we all deserve grace. You just get me.

To my mom and sisters, you are not only my God-given family but my chosen friends. I love each of you to the moon and back. Thank you for your love and support in this crazy thing we call life. It's been a joy to share it with you since day one.

——————— NOTES ———————

The Burden of a Dream

1. Andy Stanley, as quoted at Catalyst Dallas 2013

2. Tom Rath, *StrengthFinder 2.0* (Gallup Press 2007)

3. Oswald Chambers, *My Utmost for His Highest* (Discovery House Publishers 1992)

4. Jon Acuff tweet March 5, 2013

5. Jess Connolly, as quoted Influence Conference 2014

DREAM DEFENDERS UNITE

We want to celebrate your dreams and the journey you are on!

@thewellstudio
#prayersforthedreamer

{well} thewellstudio.co  @thewellstudio

We invite you to visit us online at **The {well} Studio** and gather
with us as we encourage, inspire and equip fellow dreamers,
doers and entrepreneurs on their journeys.
We desire to extend grace to ourselves and others
and instead of trying to do it all – we simply desire
to work, live and love well...*not perfectly, but {well}.*

'Well done, my good and faithful servant.
You have been faithful in handling this small amount,
so now I will give you many more responsibilities.
Let's celebrate together!'

Matthew 25:21 (NLT)

SHE DESIGNS A LIFE FULL OF DREAMS
ONLY ONE CAN FULFILL
SHE FINDS VALUE IN BEING HIS INSTEAD OF BEING BUSY
HER PASSION IS CONTAGIOUS
SHE MEASURES HERSELF IN STRENGTH, NOT POUNDS
SHE TRUSTS THE STRUGGLE
AND BREATHES IN THE JOY OF THE JOURNEY
HER STORY IS ONE TO BE HEARD
SHE RUNS FROM COMPARISON INTO THE
ARMS OF CONFIDENCE
SHE TURNS HER BACK ON PERFECTION AND
she chooses grace

THE dreamer + THE doer

PRAYER JOURNAL

This lined journal is the perfect
companion to the Thirty-one Days of
Prayer for the Dreamer + the Doer
devotional. We have designed a
unique layout that helps you brain
dump those distractions, record
your dreams & ideas, and keep
your prayers flowing on each page.

★*Order online at*
thewellstudio.co/journal

CPSIA information can be obtained at www.ICGtesting.com
Printed in the USA
LVOW02s2022010415

432944LV00012B/65/P

9 780990 965251